ABOUT THE AUTHOR

KU-270-214

When I was a little boy, they called me a liar, but now I am grown up, they call me a writer—Isaac Bashevis Singer.

Born in 1951 in Halifax, Yorks, Graham Jones was educated at Queen Elizabeth Grammar School, Wakefield, and Keble College, Oxford, where he read PPE. Since then he has worked in journalism, holding staff jobs on *The Star*, Sheffield, the *Glasgow Herald, The Sun, Now!* magazine, the *Daily Mail* and the *Daily Telegraph*. He lives with his wife Lynne, dog Rosie, cat Poppy, goldfish and visiting frogs in Hertfordshire. This is his first book.

FORKED TONGUES

The Book of Lies, Half Truths and Excuses

Graham Jones

To Jan,

Those of us with subtle
humour will appreciate this!

Happy 21st!

Anna.

29.10.84

CENTURY PUBLISHING
LONDON

The author would like to thank the publishers of
Britain's nine national daily and eight national
Sunday newspapers, the four main international news
magazines, eight British weeklies and a plethora of
British and American publishers too numerous to
mention here for providing the raw material for
Forked Tongues, but the biggest thank you of all
must go to the forked tonguesters quoted, without
whom . . .

Copyright © Graham Jones 1984
All rights reserved
First published in Great Britain in 1984
by Century Publishing Co. Ltd,
Portland House, 12–13 Greek St,
London W1V 5LE

British Library Cataloguing in Publication Data

Jones, Graham
  Forked tongues.
  1. English wit and humor
  I. Title
  828′.91407′08   PN6175

ISBN 0 7126 0331 X

Printed in Great Britain in 1984 by
The Guernsey Press Ltd,
Guernsey, Channel Islands

DEDICATION

This book is dedicated to the only people to whom I cannot lie, for they know too much – my bankers. To the managerial staff of Williams and Glyn's Bank, Church Street, Sheffield, for their patience and forbearance over the years. And in the hope this book may be good news for all of us.

CONTENTS

INTRODUCTION

The aim of the liar is to charm, to delight, to give pleasure. He is the very basis of a civilised society—Oscar Wilde.

The lie is a condition of life—Nietzche.

We all tell lies. Adults, as many as 200 a day, according to the latest research – that's 73 000 a year. Most are harmless white lies. But some in 'high risk' professions – politicians, salesmen, lawyers – find themselves habitual twisters of the truth.

This book is almost entirely composed of lies. And it's meant that way. Black lies, white lies, pink lies, blue lies. Here is every form of human deception – from the mendacity of international rogues and tyrants, through the bull of politicians and the publicity stunts of movie stars, to false protestations of modesty by the gentle and the good.

It's a testament to human folly. A warning to all who say 'they'll never know' or 'nobody will ever find out'. In all, here are more than 1000 examples of lies, doublespeak, bogus denials and false promises. A few of the lie lines are old favourites. But most have been winkled out and awarded their true – or, should we say, untrue – place in history for the very first time.

You'll never know who to believe again!

1
A WORLD OF UNTRUTHS

'All men are born truthful, and die liars,' wrote
Vauvenargues. And then at least he was telling the truth. For
everyone at some time or other speaks with a forked tongue.
It's not whether, it's when. It's just a question of how big the
lies, how often – and the damage they do.

I do not expect to be impeached and I will not
resign.

President Richard Nixon, February 1974

No woman in my time will be Prime Minister or
Foreign Secretary – not the top jobs. Anyway, I
wouldn't want to be Prime Minister. You have to
give yourself one hundred per cent.

Margaret Thatcher, October 1969

There is not a shred of doubt that the documents
and diaries are genuine.

> *Gerd Heidemann of* Stern *magazine on the*
> *'Hitler Diaries'*

It was a quiet sort of evening. A convivial evening,
much like when one would have friends round in
this country. It was not remarkable in any way.

> *Dr Richard Arnot at the Helen Smith*
> *inquest, December 1982*

Together we're going to do what has to be done.
Together we're going to put America to work
again.

> *Ronald Reagan, presidential victory*
> *speech, November 1980*

There is going to be no axeing from TV-am. No
one is going to be kicked out and no one is going
to walk the plank.

> *David Frost, March 1983*

It may be an honest slip-up.

I ask you to join me in a toast to President
Figueiredo and the people of Bolivia . . . no, that's
where I'm going.

> *Ronald Reagan, in Brazil, December 1982.*
> *(Wrong again! His next stop was Bogota,*
> *Colombia)*

I'd like to extend a warm welcome to Chairman
Mo.

> *Oh dear. Ronald Reagan again. He meant*
> President Doe *of Liberia*

It may be protective. A doctor wanting to aid his patient's
recovery. A government acting to prevent a disastrous run on
a nation's currency. The armed forces deceiving the enemy to
try to save lives.

We did not tell lies. But we did not tell the whole story.

> *Sir Frank Cooper, British defence chief, on*
> *the Falklands*

It may be bad crystal-ball gazing.

> The world of today is a bare, hungry, dilapidated place compared with the world that existed before 1914.
>
> *George Orwell,* 1984

Khomeini? No one refers to him in Iran except the terrorists.

> *Shah of Iran*

I think that some of the experts rather exaggerate the rôle, the strength, of the Argentine air force.
> *British Defence Secretary John Nott*

But more likely the motives are less straightforward.

> I will never, *never* trade my Senate seat for the Vice-Presidency.
>
> *Lyndon B. Johnson*

There can be no whitewash at the White House.
> *Richard Nixon*

These are the worst type of falsehood. Monsters, whoppers.

> I have nothing to hide.
>
> *Spiro Agnew*

The Soviet Union does not intend to interfere in the affairs of other countries. Every people decides its own destiny.
> *Yuri Andropov, Soviet KGB boss, before*
> *Afghanistan and Poland*

5

We did more than any historian ever did before who published documents.

Peter Koch, editor-in-chief, Stern *magazine, about the 'Hitler Diaries'*

I want to live in peace with England and conclude a definite pact; to guarantee all the English possessions in the world and to collaborate.

Adolf Hitler, August 1939

The Polish situation is developing in a very positive way.

Vadim Zagladin, deputy chief of the Soviet foreign ministry, January 1983

Rather less worthy of scorn are the white lies we all tell from time to time. Though few could beat the First Lord of the fib, Admiral Horatio Nelson. Ordered to retreat during the Battle of Copenhagen in 1801, he hoisted that famous telescope to his blind eye, declaring:

I have only one eye. I have a right to be blind
sometimes . . . . I really do not see the signal.

I am being frank about myself in this book. I tell
of my first mistake on page 850.

Henry Kissinger

No, I'm not disappointed – I'm actually rather
pleased in a way. This truly is a remarkable result.

*Shirley Williams, losing at Crosby, June
1983*

Every remark cannot neatly be classified 'black' or 'white',
of course. There's a murky middle ground.

The situation in Vietnam is very, very encouraging.

General Westmoreland, 1967

He meant for the North Vietnamese.

There have been improvements in security at the
palace over the past 18 months.

*Home Secretary Willie Whitelaw
announcing the Queen's bedroom break-in*

Balancing your budget is like protecting your
virtue – you have to learn to say no.

Ronald Reagan, January 1980

So he said no to balancing his budget!
  Mind you, you know what Disraeli said: There are lies,
damned lies, and statistics.

Peter Tatchell (Labour)	41.4%
John O'Grady (Real Bermondsey Labour)	8.7%
Robert Hughes (Conservative)	3.6%
Simon Hughes (Liberal-SDP Alliance)	3.5%

*Labour eve-of-poll forecast to press
'having canvassed 68 per cent of the
Bermondsey electorate'*

In 1984 Disraeli would probably say there are lies, damned statistics – and doublespeak. It's the new way to lie – trying to deceive by verbal smokescreen. And today it's a multinational growth industry. Thank the military:

> You always write it's bombing, bombing. It's not bombing. It's air support.
> *Col. H.E. Opfer, USAF attaché, Phnom Penh,*
> *winner of the 1974 US Doublespeak award*

In 1983 the Reagan administration were calling a US-backed invasion of Nicaragua in retaliation for Communist insurgency in El Salvador:

> Symmetry.

Though the real champ was always former Secretary of State Alexander Haig. To an aide asking for a pay rise:

> HAIG: Because of the fluctuational predispositions of your position's productive capacity as juxtaposed to government standards, it would be momentarily injudicious to advocate an increment.
> AIDE: I don't get it.
> HAIG: That's right!

This kind of duplicity does have its lighter side.

> I have the thermometer in my mouth and I am listening to it all the time. *Willie Whitelaw*

> In Israel, in order to be a realist you have to believe in miracles. *David Ben-Gurion*

Some people do tend to talk through their hats.

> I would decry the notion that there is a recession.
> *Mark Thatcher, April 1982*

> We've taken six weeks to do what the BBC has taken 50 years to do. We're all hacks, but they're

real hacks. We know what's going to happen before it happens, we won't just react to news . . . .

Tim Holdin, reporter, on the launch of TV-am

I say categorically that I have no contemplation at all of being the candidate for anything in 1964, 1966, 1968 or 1972. Anybody who thinks I would be a candidate for anything in any year is off his rocker.

Richard Nixon, 1963

It's ridiculous to imagine that I have any idea of marrying the King.

Mrs Wallis Simpson, 1936

Baseball — what's that? Whoever made a living outa baseball?

Papa DiMaggio to millionaire-star-to-be Joe DiMaggio

You can forget about OPEC. They will never amount to a row of beans.

Senior Ministry of Power official, 1967, quoted by Lord Robens

If in doubt, look for an official denial.

There is no romance and there are no grounds for these rumours of a romance between Lieutenant Mark Phillips and myself. I cannot understand why there is all this interest in our going riding together.

Princess Anne, March 1973

Laker Airways are perfectly healthy. Rumours of the airline going bankrupt are malicious and fictitious. There is absolutely no question of the airline folding. The only liquidation around Gatwick is the rain.

Laker Airways spokesman, January 1982, 16 days before the airline crashed owing 350 million dollars

> Can I say that the individual concerned is not an endorsed candidate of the Labour Party, and as far as I am concerned, never will be.
>
> *Michael Foot on Peter Tatchell*

Things do change, of course. What is known in politics as a slight alteration in the prevailing circumstances. Or, to the rest of us, a complete U-turn.

> If I have anything to do with it, any handover of power to the Patriotic Front will not take place.
>
> *Ian Smith, 6 July 1977*

> If we find Ian Smith alive when we take power, he will be tried by a People's Court, and, I hope, shot.
>
> *Robert Mugabe, 30 March 1978*

Then when he did take power:

> I have met with Mr Smith and we agreed to co-operate.
>
> *Robert Mugabe, 5 March 1980*

Of course, the memory sometimes plays tricks. Or that's what the politicians would say.

> I took part in the Grunwick picket line five weeks ago on May 19. I joined in because I thought my union, Apex, was perfectly right on the merits of the dispute.
>
> *Shirley Williams, 1977*

> Well, I wasn't part of the picket line. I visited those who were picketing.
>
> *Shirley Williams, 1979*

Show business is another profession full of forked tongues.

> TV-am is bloody rubbish, shabby, unprofessional, and garbage. I can't work there any more.
>
> *Michael Parkinson, 20 April 1983*
> *(morning)*

I am glad to be staying on. I was very happy with what Timothy Aitken said and I would like to be part of that progress.

> *Michael Parkinson, 20 April 1983*
> *(afternoon)*

As Sean Connery said:

I'll never play Bond again.

> *After* You Only Live Twice

Then:

I'll never play Bond again.

> *After* Diamonds are Forever

Small wonder they called his next Bond film *Never Say Never Again*. But others, too, have been known to live their lives on the 'never never'.

Man will never fly. Not in a thousand years.

> *Wilbur Wright, 1900*

I don't believe in majority rule ever in Rhodesia. Not in a thousand years.

> *Ian Smith, March 1976*

At no time have I contemplated, sought, proposed, or recommended, or been asked by the Prime Minister to contemplate, seek, propose or recommend any cut in the published defence budget of the United Kingdom.

> *John Nott, Defence Secretary, May 1981*

They did cut defence, and then came the Falklands.
  Which brings us on to another sort of defensive shot – the excuse we all use from time to time.

I helped Ronald Reagan's presidency. When I shot him, his polls went up 30 per cent.

> *John Hinckley Jnr*

I've done a hard day's work for the Queen. It may be I've done her a favour.

> *Palace intruder Michael Fagan (he lied about his name and address too, saying he was 'Rudolph Hess from Spandau')*

All I was ever concerned about was the workforce in Northern Ireland.

> *John De Lorean*

From the Israeli point of view, it is the most humane siege of a city imaginable.

> *Izchak Ben-Ari, Israeli Ambassador to West Germany, on the bombing of Beirut, July 1982*

There is, however, one type of liar who invokes respect, not bullets. False modesty does afflict some truly great men.

I have offended against God and mankind because
my work did not reach the quality it should have.

Leonardo da Vinci, dying words

Though it seems to affect women even worse:

To put it bluntly, I seem to be a whole
superstructure without a foundation.

Marilyn Monroe

I'm quite insignificant really.

Raquel Welch

God, I'm such a short arse.

Glenda Jackson

Needless to say, there are those whose opinions of themselves
tend towards the other direction:

I myself consider I am the most powerful figure in
the world.

Idi Amin

I am in a great state of euphoria. I have just given the finest party political broadcast in history.
Harold Wilson, 1976, quoted by Richard Crossman

Some people are known for, well, double standards.

It is vital, in my opinion, that tennis maintains a strong and watchful stand against swearing.
John McEnroe

We are confident that our presence in Lebanon has saved thousands of human lives.
Yitzhak Shamir, Israeli Foreign Minister

No member has the right to join the Labour party and then say, 'Ah, there are some things I don't go along with.'
Robert Mellish, MP, who later left the Labour Party

Time is a great revealer, especially where the truth is concerned.

IT'S AN OCTOBER ELECTION!
The general election will NOT be held in June.
Instead, I can reveal, Premier Margaret Thatcher is
planning the poll in October.

> *Victor Knight, political editor,* Sunday
> Mirror, *May 1983*

The forthcoming general election will be the most
open battle in recent political history. The
conclusions of the opinion polls are meaningless.

> *Roy Hattersley, March 1983*

Travel is no problem in 1984. There are no
bottlenecks or intersections. The wide motorway
leapfrogs across the countryside on stilts, beneath
which speed the trains which have taken the freight
off the roads to give the motorists a clear run.

> *Ronald Brech, statistician, writing in 1963*

In 1984 the Arts, in any historical meaning of the
word, will have disappeared . . . there will be lights
everywhere except in the mind of man, and the fall
of the last civilisation will not be heard above the
incessant din.

> *Sir Herbert Read, writing in 1964*

All the presenters are staying at TV-am. I think the
'Famous Five' are a tremendous asset to the
company.

> *Jonathan Aitken*

ONLY A LABOUR MAN CAN WIN, BUT WHICH ONE?
When Bermondsey votes on February 24, only a
Labour candidate can win the seat.

> *Joe Haines,* Daily Mirror

Don't panic, we're here to stay.

> *Peter Jay to TV-am staff, March 1983*

As Bjorn Borg said:

> A single-minded and ambitious man has no time for a steady girlfriend, not to mention marriage, if he is to succeed as a tennis player.
>
> *Autobiography, 1975*

He did manage to fit Mariana in, between those five wins at Wimbledon.

> Television? No good will come of this device. The word is half Greek and half Latin.
>
> *C.P. Scott*

> My dear Kuhn, English kings don't abdicate.
>
> *Senior British diplomat to Ferdinand Kuhn*
> *Jnr of the* New York Times, *1936*

> *Gone with the Wind* is going to be the biggest flop in Hollywood history. I'm just glad it'll be Clark Gable who's falling flat on his face and not me.
>
> *Gary Cooper*

And not forgetting Kay Graham, publisher of the *Washington Post*. When told on 17 June 1972 of comic-opera burglars caught in the Democratic Party HQ in the Watergate building, Mrs Graham asked one of her executives, in a classic one-liner:

> Is there no *serious* news today?

2
FORKED TONGUES

'Ask me no questions, and I'll tell you no fibs,' wrote Oliver Goldsmith. 'No man speaks the truth or leads a true life for two minutes together,' said Ralph Waldo Emerson. And remember Mark Twain: 'A lie can travel round the world while the truth is putting on its shoes.'

This, then, is the world of Forked Tongues:

Q. Mr Foot, do you believe you'll win tomorrow?
A. Yes, we do indeed.

> *Michael Foot, ITN news, 8 June 1983. (He later said he knew all along he'd lose)*

The Governor has asked me to reiterate what he has said on many occasions – he is not a candidate for President or any other national office.

> *Ronald Reagan's secretary, 1969*

I declare unequivocally I will not accept the Vice-Presidential nomination.

> *George Bush, 1980*

I will seek no tax increases this year.

> *Ronald Reagan, 1982*

He then announced the second biggest tax hike in US history.

I have Michael Foot beaten. Already I have warned Michael sadly, that I have him beaten.

> *John Silkin, Labour leadership contender, October 1980. He came a poor third*

CHARLES TO MARRY ASTRID – OFFICIAL
Prince Charles is to marry Princess Marie-Astrid of Luxembourg. The formal announcement will be made from Buckingham Palace next Monday.

> Daily Express *splash story, June 1977*

I would never say anything against the Royal Family.

> *Kieran Kenny, former Royal servant who sold his story to* The Sun. *After revelations of how 'Queen Koo Romped at Palace' a writ was issued. The next instalment, 'Barefoot Di buttered my Toast' failed to appear*

By now I had expected to be heaped with accolades, possibly to be knighted by the Queen.

> *(Sir) John De Lorean, 1982*

If present trends continue, by 1984 the average male wage would amount to £2000 a year.

> *Lord Hailsham, 1961*

Gosh!

In 1984, it's a far quieter world. There are no rattling pneumatic drills. For road works we use sound waves too high for the ear to receive. Space is rather taken for granted. Mining trucks ply between Earth and asteroids, those tiny planets orbiting the Sun between Mars and Jupiter. They bring us silver, lead, zinc and some minerals unknown 20 years ago. Only occasionally is a space train missing. We live longer and better than ever before thanks to these new wonder anti-virus drugs. Most kinds of cancer can be cured . . . .

> *Noel Lindblom, science writer, 1963*

Talking of cancers:

We neither of us have ever been Communist agents.

> *Guy Burgess and Donald Maclean, joint statement, 1956*

THE USSR: THE BULWARK OF THE GREAT CAUSE OF PEACE AND FREEDOM OF NATIONS

> *Subheading, report to the Central Committee by Yuri Andropov, December 1982*

War is peace, freedom is slavery, ignorance is strength.

This was an unprecedented accident. It was not at all the fault of the Soviets.

> *Col. Semyon Romanov, chief of Soviet air defences, on the Korean Airlines 747, September 1983*

The Labour Party is and always has been an instinctive part of my life.

> *Roy Jenkins, March 1973*

We believe that a centre party would have no roots, no principles, no philosophy and no values.

> *Shirley Williams, 1980, before she left the Labour Party*

I'm not glad this tour is over. I've enjoyed it very much.

> *England cricket captain Bob Willis after disastrous tour of Australia and New Zealand, 1982/83*

I was proud of them. They were hit by two sucker goals, and they showed tremendous character in the way they kept fighting back. I do not think they could have played much better.

> *Sir Alf Ramsey, 1973, after England were trounced 2−0 in Poland, on the way to being eliminated from the World Cup*

JAP PLANE CARRIER AND FOUR U-BOATS SUNK

> Daily Express *headline on Pearl Harbour, giving victory to the wrong side (though blame US defence spokesmen)*

Concorde was never intended to be a 'prestige product' or the world's most expensive status symbol. It is designed to make money for its operators and manufacturers.

> *T.E. Blackall, Concorde biographer, 1969*

I'm not contemplating any changes. It would be the easiest thing in the world to sack Terry Neill and I'm not convinced that is the right answer.

Peter Hill-Wood, chairman of Arsenal
F.C., 2 December, 1983

Less than two weeks later, Mr Hill-Wood sacked Terry Neill.

This is my last concert. I have retired.

Frank Sinatra, Los Angeles, June 1971

But if he didn't keep retiring, who'd want to go to his comebacks?

By 1984 poetry, already an arcane activity, will have totally disappeared. Fiction, even now a diminishing form of entertainment, will fade out and the only writers will be script-writers for the television screen.

Sir Herbert Read, 1964

Who would make such rash predictions . . . .

The people talk very high of their power to resist Great Britain; but it is all talk.

Sir Francis Bernard, British Governor of
Massachusetts, 1766 (shortly before the
American War of Independence)

But you know the 'colonial mentality'. In 1952, the year a state of emergency was declared in Kenya and the Mau Mau began in earnest their campaign of terror which was to claim 13 000 lives, the Colonial Office annual report on the territory concluded:

Of all the events of the year, the most memorable is the visit to the colony of Her Majesty the Queen and His Royal Highness the Duke of Edinburgh . . . . They visited the Pumwani Maternity Hospital and attended a Garden Party at Government House . . . .

James Callaghan will never be Prime Minister of Britain.

> *Robert Muldoon, Prime Minister of New Zealand*

The question of Cecil Parkinson's resignation does not – and will not – arise.

> *10 Downing Street spokesman, 5 October 1983*

We're being clobbered.

> *Bobby Kennedy, 1960, at first presidential election results from Kentucky. His brother John went on to win*

FORD IS REAGAN'S RUNNING MATE

> *Announcement on three TV networks and splash story in the* Chicago Sun-Times, *Detroit, 1980*

But that's the US Presidency. On 15 October 1962, when the great drama of the Cuban missile crisis was unfolding unknown to the world, President John Kennedy interrupted a political tour in Chicago. His spokesman announced:

> The President is returning to Washington to consult his doctors. He has a cold.

Meanwhile, Vice-President Johnson interrupted his political tour in Hawaii. His spokesman announced:

> The Vice-President is returning to Washington to consult his doctors. He has a cold.

One famous US journalist realised there was more to it than that. He checked, and sure enough, a plethora of top White House, State Department, and Pentagon officials were away from their desks, suffering from a variety of ailments. He realised he had a big story on his hands.

The intrepid newsman rang the White House to get the final evidence for his 'scoop'. Calmly, he told them he knew everything.

I know what you're trying to hide from us. There's been an epidemic!

Well, an epidemic of lies, at least.

My brother will be remembered as a great art historian.
> *Wilfred Blunt, brother of Anthony*

We only wish to pursue our work with honour and peace!
> *Dr Joseph Goebbels*

I am a man of honour who has been misunderstood all my life. My organisation has been misunderstood. It is a beautiful symbol of my tradition.
> *Mafia chieftain Joe Bonanno*

There's no way I will allow Brando to play the Don. He'll keep people out of the cinemas.
> *Paramount executive on* The Godfather

In the marginal constituencies we are doing magnificently. We really are doing very well.
> *Michael Foot, 8 June 1983*

Iran will need a King for a long time yet.
> *Empress Farah Diba of Iran, 1978*

We will be here for ever now.
> *Gen. Oswaldo Garcia, Argentine commander on the Falklands*

3
THE QUEEN OF CAPRICE

'It's a woman's prerogative to change her mind,' runs the popular saying. And if woman's ability to do a quick about-turn has produced in itself a whole farrago of forked tongues, one woman stands head and shoulders above the rest in the art: Elizabeth Taylor.

BOYFRIEND No. 1 – Lieut. GLENN DAVIS
I'm going to wait for Glenn and we'll marry when I'm eighteen or nineteen. We're engaged to be engaged. I love Glenn and I want to be with him.

1948. He went to Korea

FIANCÉ No. 1 – BILL PAWLEY
Just as soon as I get this picture finished then we'll get married. I'd rather make babies than movies.

1949. She decided she liked making pictures after all

HUSBAND No. 1 – NICKY HILTON
Your heart knows when you meet the right man. There is no doubt that Nicky is the one I want to spend my life with.

May 1950. Divorced

HUSBAND No. 2 – MICHAEL WILDING
I just want to be with Michael, to be his wife. He enjoys sitting home, smoking his pipe, reading, painting. And that's what I intend doing – all except smoking a pipe.
This is, for me, the beginning of a happy end.

February 1952. Divorced

HUSBAND No. 3 – MIKE TODD
I have given him my eternal love . . . . This marriage will last forever. For me it will be third time lucky.

I am far more interested in being Mrs Michael Todd than in being an actress.

February 1957. He died March 1958

HUSBAND No. 4 – EDDIE FISHER
I have never been happier in my life . . . . We will be on our honeymoon for 30 or 40 years.

May 1959. An inscription on an anniversary present from her to him read 'I love and need you with my life for the rest of time.' The marriage was dissolved when Elizabeth Taylor met Richard Burton

HUSBAND No. 5 – RICHARD BURTON (1st)
I'm so happy you can't believe it . . . . I love him enough to stand by him, no matter what he might do and I would want.

March 1964. They divorced in June 1974

HUSBAND No. 6 – RICHARD BURTON (2nd)
The separation was inevitable. It had to happen to make what we have got now.

There will be no more bloody marriages or divorces. We are stuck like chicken feathers to tar – for lovely always.

October 1975. Soon afterwards, they divorced again

HUSBAND No. 7 – JOHN WARNER
I feel as if I've come home to nest. John is the best lover I've ever had . . . . I want to spend the rest of my life with him and I want to be buried with him. I don't think of him as husband number seven. He's number one all the way.

December 1976. They separated in December 1981

FIANCÉ No. 8 – VICTOR LUNA
I am really in love.

On their engagement, August 1983

Elizabeth's about-turn on Senator Warner was typical of more than 30 years of volte-face.

> The difference in this marriage is the extra effort we both put in. It's not a 50-50 proposition but a 51-51.
>
> *Liz on John Warner, 1976*

> There was nothing for me to do except stay at home and watch the boob tube. Life had no meaning, no responsibility.
>
> *Liz on John Warner, 1982*

And there was an astonishing public U-turn in February 1982 when fate brought both Taylor's and Burton's shows to London's West End. At first she insisted:

> I won't be seeing Richard Burton. I'm a lady on the loose.
>
> *24 February 1982*

Then she took to the stage in a public display of kissing and cuddling with the Welsh actor, cooing:

> We have always been in love.
>
> *28 February 1982*

There was such dazzling publicity for both of them, one has to ask: is Liz always being honest when she's not telling the truth?

Certainly some of the Taylor ways seemed to have rubbed off on Richard Burton over the years.

Under the headline I WON'T MARRY LIZ! Sheilah Graham ran an interview with Burton in May 1962 quoting him:

> There's no chance of me announcing I am divorcing my wife to marry Elizabeth.

According to Sheilah Graham, Burton told her:

> I shall never leave Sybil. She loves and understands me and thinks I'm a genius.

Meanwhile Sybil Burton, too, had caught the bug. She was saying:

> Liz Taylor? I adore her. She's an old friend of mine.

And:

> My marriage to Richard is fine, just fine, thank you very much.

The on-off Taylor-Burton saga was later to produce a memorable press statement from Liz's PR aide John Springer. Asked in June 1973 about rumours the couple were parting, he declared:

> The only thing I can say is that nobody else is involved if there is a split temporarily or otherwise and I'm not admitting there is.

Richard Burton, too, wasn't prepared to tell the truth – that their marriage was on the rocks.

> I even have Elizabeth's passport in my possession. Does that sound as though she's left me?

Burton went through the same routine when he separated from his fourth wife, Suzy Hunt.

> All is serene. They spend hours on the telephone talking to each other every day. These stories have cropped up before and there is nothing in it.
> *Burton spokeswoman Valerie Douglas,*
> *13 February 1982*

> The six-year marriage is over. Suzy will be suing for divorce.
> *Burton spokeswoman Nancy Selzer,*
> *20 February 1982*

Surprise, surprise, the previous eight months had seen the same firm denials from Liz's PR aides over her marriage to John Warner.

Mr and Mrs Warner are very much together.
> *Taylor spokesman B.J. Wilkins, June 1981*

Don't believe a word of it. It just can't be true. The rumours are totally without foundation.
> *Taylor spokeswoman Chen Sam, December 1981*

The split from Senator Warner was announced officially just one day later!

In February 1983, it was the same all over again. A 'close friend' of Liz this time talked to the press. There was a firm denial there would be any engagement to Victor Luna:

They like being together. But no one believes there is more to it than that.

But the odd lie or two has been known to crop up in the Elizabeth Taylor story.

It's just a bauble.
> *Richard Burton on buying the world's most expensive diamond – for $1 million – at Cartiers', October 1969*

I threw Elizabeth out, told her to get out – and to my surprise she went. I couldn't believe it.
> *Richard Burton, 1973*

All this stuff about Elizabeth being the most beautiful woman in the world is absolute nonsense. She's pretty enough and her eyes are nice but she has an insipid double chin, big feet, stumpy legs, a pot belly, and she's as pouty-breasted as a pigeon.
> *Richard Burton, 1965*

When you consider that men have always let her down, you realise what a tough married life she's had.
> *Richard Burton, 1975*

Elizabeth was the only wife to drive a man to milk.
Richard Burton, 1983

Though perhaps the last word should go to Liz Taylor's mother Sara, generally credited as being the most determined stage mother ever to hit Hollywood.

We didn't want her in pictures. We just wanted her to have a normal life.

4
THE WORLD'S TOP TWENTY LIES

1 Sorry
2 I love you
3 I'm on a diet
4 Pleased to meet you
5 How interesting
6 You look great
7 Honestly
8 I didn't realise the time
9 I couldn't get away
10 We're just good friends
11 Very good condition
12 A bargain
13 It's not the money
14 I'm on £20 000/£25 000/£30 000 a year
15 I wouldn't fancy America/the Greek Islands/the Caribbean
16 There's nothing on TV worth watching

17 I couldn't eat another thing
18 Just a quick cup of coffee
19 I've never done this kind of thing before
20 Everything will be all right

5
MONSTERS, WHOPPERS – DO YOU BELIEVE THEM?

'In the big lie there is always a certain force of credibility,' wrote Adolf Hitler in *Mein Kampf*. And from his place in history as prince of tyrants, dictators and despots, no one can have known better.

It wasn't always so. According to Jonathan Swift, 'As universal a practice as lying is, and easy a one as it seems, I do not remember to have heard three good lies in all my conversations, even from those who were most celebrated in that faculty.'

Well, he did live before Nixon.

> Let us begin by committing ourselves to the truth, to see it like it is and to tell it like it is, to find the truth, to speak the truth and to live with the truth. That's what we'll do.
>
> *Richard Nixon, Republican nomination acceptance speech, Miami, August 1968*

> The White House has no involvement in this particular incident.
>
> *Richard Nixon on the Watergate break-in, White House press conference, June 1972*

> I can't give you the names of those who supplied the diaries. Lives would be endangered.
>
> *Gerd Heidemann of* Stern *magazine, on the 'Hitler Diaries'*

> We want war with no nation.
>
> *Yoshuke Matsuoka, Japanese Foreign Minister 1940–41*

> Miss Keeler and I were on friendly terms. There was no impropriety whatsoever in my relationship with Miss Keeler.
>
> *War Secretary John Profumo, 1963*

An isolated band of renegades . . . their actions are the result of political and ideological aberrations, religious fanaticism, nationality quirks, personality failures and resentment and in many cases mental instability.

Yuri Andropov on dissidents

I will maintain this resolution, even if it is my ruin: I will sign no document with a mental reservation not to fulfil it. What I sign I will stand by. What I cannot stand by, I will not sign.

Adolf Hitler's new diplomacy, 1933, after withdrawing from the Disarmament Conference and the League of Nations

The trouble was, Chamberlain believed him.
Others have been just as quick to put pen to paper.

I promise Patricia Ryan Nixon that I will not again seek public office.

Richard M. Nixon, 1952

In our country it is not forbidden 'to think differently' from the majority, to criticise different aspects of public life. We regard the comrades who come out with well-founded criticism, who strive for improvement, as well-intentioned critics, and we are grateful to them.

Leonid Brezhnev, 1977

Soviet planes tried to give the aircraft assistance in directing it to the nearest airfield.

First two-paragraph statement from Tass, implicitly denying the Soviets had shot down a Korean jumbo jet, September 1983

You're the best supporters in the country and we're the most attack-minded team.

Allan Clarke to Leeds United fans, 1982

31

If he had contacted me, everything would have
been all right.
Idi Amin on the resignation of Lord
Carrington

Argentina had no choice but to take over the
Malvinas. Britain had closed all doors open to
negotiation on the basic issue of sovereignty.
Argentine government spokesman after the
Franks report, January 1983

I know for certain that we had no troops in the area.
Phalangist militia spokesman after the
Beirut massacres

There are not going to be any landings or anything
like that. This is not to be construed as a
provocative act.
Pentagon spokesman on the US Navy Task
Force steaming towards Grenada, October
1983

I don't think this visit has caused offence to anyone.
Ken Livingstone, GLC leader, on inviting
two top Sinn Fein leaders to London

We do not wish to impose a Communist regime in
Saigon. What we want is the establishment of a
three segment government of national concord.
Le Duc Tho, Hanoi's chief negotiator at
Paris, 1972

The disappearance of the British diplomats Burgess
and Maclean and Mrs Maclean has not the slightest
connection with the Soviet Union.
Soviet journal New Times, *1953*

There has been a motor accident.
Idi Amin, on the death of Archbishop
Janan Luwuum and two cabinet ministers
(his men machine-gunned them to death,
then faked a crash)

Remember the Nazis' 'shot trying to escape'?

> German National Socialists are gladly prepared to
> make a great and valuable contribution to universal
> world peace.
>
> *Dr Joseph Goebbels, German Propaganda*
> *Minister, 1937*

> The Germans did not want this war. It was forced
> upon us because the enemy powers were not
> prepared to permit us to be independent and knew
> very well that independence would give our nation
> unprecedented strength and vigour.
>
> *Dr Joseph Goebbels, 1939*

To some, it's always the other side's fault:

> A fateful hour has fallen for Germany. Envious
> peoples everywhere are compelling us to our just
> defence. The sword has been forced into our hands.
>
> *Kaiser Wilhelm, August 1914*

Really, they wouldn't hurt a fly.

> I'm just a harmless mental patient who wouldn't
> hurt a fly, President Reagan, or Jodie Foster.
>
> *John Hinckley Jnr*

> We always exert ourselves the utmost to improve
> our relationships with the United States of America.
>
> *Col. Muammar Gaddafi*

> My people know that everything that was told
> against me was lies.
>
> *Idi Amin*

> Our coming to our neighbour – at his urgent
> request – is not aggression or intervention, as ill-
> intentioned slanderers try to prove. The only task
> before the Soviet military contingent is to help
> Afghanistan repel the threat from outside.
>
> Red Star, *Soviet army newspaper*

I don't believe in the depression, it's a myth.
> *David Wickins, chairman of British Car*
> *Auctions, 1982*

We declare with a full sense of responsibility: we
have no territorial claims on anyone whatsoever, we
threaten no one, and have no intention of attacking
anyone, we stand for the free and independent
development of all nations.
> *Leonid Brezhnev, 1971*

Our problem at the moment is one of success.
> *Edward Heath, 1973*

I don't think you can dismiss these people as
extremists and terrorists.
> *Ken Livingstone on Sinn Fein, political*
> *wing of the IRA*

No state in the world campaigns for peace with
more energy and dedication than the Soviet Union
does.
> *East German government statement*

I have always been so frightfully proper.
> *Mandy Rice-Davies, who scandalised*
> *Britain in the Profumo affair*

MALVINAS – WE REPELLED THEM
THROUGH BLOOD AND FIRE
The invasion attempts on the islands have failed
and the enemy forces suffered heavy losses.
> Cronica, *Argentine newspaper, May 1982*

Soviet fraternal assistance in Czechoslovakia
strengthened the positions of socialism and peace in
Europe and the world.
> *Czech government statement on the*
> *fifteenth anniversary of the Soviet*
> *invasion, 1983*

I hate war. And if the day comes when my vote must be cast to send your boy to war, that day Lyndon Johnson will leave his seat in Congress and go with him.

Lyndon B. Johnson, 1941

Perhaps he couldn't book a flight.

The very term 'dissident' is a witty propaganda invention used to mislead the public. Those who are misled, we try to help. We try to educate them, to disperse their delusions.

Yuri Andropov

Britain can achieve in the seventies what Germany and France achieved in the fifties and sixties.

Denis Healey, Chancellor of the Exchequer, 1976

He was always a Silly Billy.

There are no permanent enemies in politics.

Idi Amin

Especially if you kill them.

Real progress has been made in finding out the truth.

Richard Nixon on Watergate, April 1973

The Soviet Union and other socialist states decided to meet the request of Czechoslovak party leaders and statesmen to render urgent assistance to the fraternal Czechoslovak people, including assistance with armed forces. All talk of 'imposing' the 'Soviet brand' of socialism on Czechs and Slovaks is nothing else but a malicious and provocative lie.

Pravda *leading article, August 1968*

Hmm. (Incidentally, *Pravda* in Russian means truth, while *Izvestia* means news. It's a favourite Russian saying that there's no news in Izvestia, and no truth in Pravda.)

I've nothing to declare.

> *Michael Mackellar, Australian Health*
> *Minister, breezing through customs with a*
> *Hong Kong portable TV, April 1982. He*
> *was forced to resign*

JOHN LLOYD-ELEY QC, at the Old Bailey: Have you done anything prejudicial to the safety or interests of the United Kingdom?

PROF. HUGH HAMBLETON: No, Sir, I have not.

The next day Hambleton admitted he'd lied – he was a spy – and got 15 years.

Kampuchea hopes to increase its population from eight million to 15 or 20 million in the next ten years.

> *Pol Pot, October 1977*

A pity he killed more than four million in the first place.

We didn't fail. Now we're coming good.

> *John De Lorean, 1981*

I have acted according to my conscience.

> *Anthony Blunt, traitor unmasked,*
> *November 1979*

There are no Libyan troops or planes in Chad.

> *Col. Gaddafi, August 1983*

I've never been to bed with a man for money.

> *Christine Keeler, autobiography, 1968 (she*
> *later admitted it was 'a pack of lies')*

Our foreign policy is well known. It is a policy of peace and international co-operation.

> *Leonid Brezhnev*

He would have his little jokes!

6
FIBS, HALF-TRUTHS, THOSE LITTLE WHITE LIES

'Someone says it's a lie,' said Winston Churchill. 'Well I am reminded by that remark of the witty Irishman who said: "There are a terrible lot of lies going round the world, and the worst of it is that half of them are true".'

If the world is full of half-truths, it must equally be full of half-lies. Not all intended to injure, of course. There is a particular brand of dishonesty that is practised every day, every time – by everybody. The fib. White lie. That conversation breaker. Reputation maker. Face – and marriage – saver.

If we can take *The Gentleman's Magazine*'s word for it, none should feel too ashamed:

> A white lie is that which is not intended to injure any Body in his Fortune, Interest, or Reputation, but only to gratify a garrulous Disposition, and the Itch of amusing people by telling them wonderful stories.

And protecting the ego, of course. Especially when it comes to the auld enemy, age.

> Zsa Zsa Gabor is now even younger than she was last year. To complicate matters, she has now produced another birth certificate which claims she was born in February, 1928. This would make her 54. The Motion Picture Almanac says she is 59. The International Celebrity Register, not wishing to be controversial, says she was born 'circa 1920'.
>
> If Zsa Zsa is to be believed, she was only 8 when she came second in the 1936 Miss Hungary contest ('I should have come first'). Her real age: 63.
>
> Daily Mirror, *April 1982*

Screen legend Marlene Dietrich celebrates her 80th birthday this year. Or does she? One reference book of the stars lists her as approaching her 80th birthday on December 27 this year. The respected *Who's Who in the Theatre* has her coming up to 83, while other books put her at 79 and 81. Last year, Marlene herself was claiming to a mere 77 and, at the same time, her secretary in Paris said: 'She was born on 27 December 1904, and can prove it by producing her passport.' That would make the great lady 78 now. All very confusing.

Titbits, *July 1983*

Joan Collins confessed to a reporter in June 1982:

Forty-six and cross my heart.

Then, when another newspaper produced her birth certificate, she aged four years in six months and began admitting to 50. Though the evergreen Miss Collins did once say:

A woman who will tell you her age will tell you *anything*.

According to *her* official biography, Nancy Reagan was born in 1923. White House insiders say she was born on 26 July 1921. Her sixtieth birthday was very late coming.

Several years ago I was film-tested for a picture called *National Velvet*. Another girl who was three years older than me got the part. Her name is Elizabeth Taylor and now she is four years younger than me.

Shirley Williams

One thought: what if Roy Jenkins had screen-tested for *Ben-Hur*?

I must have been three when I was born.
Archie Moore, world light-heavyweight boxing champion

How old is he? Oh, 29. You know, 29, going on 33.
Soccer writer on star Manchester City forward

(Then it was his birthday. And he became 28!)

> I was born old and get younger every day.
> *Sir Herbert Beerbohm Tree*

> When people say I'm seventy I say that's a
> confounded lie. I'm twice 35, that's all. Twice 35.
> *Alfred Hitchcock*

> I'm exactly 50 years old, and have been for 25 years.
> *James Cameron*

> I'm 39. I know I have been married 38 years. I
> married at the age of one.
> *Jack Benny*

Though Eva Gabor had the best way to stop the whispers. She
used to announce:

> I'm 120.

This kind of blarney is not only used about ourselves. How
often have we heard that way-out optimistic phrase:

> Ladies and gentlemen – the next President of the
> United States!

One in a hundred or so make it. Then it's their turn to bluff.

> My great-great-grandfather died at the Alamo.
> *Lyndon B. Johnson to troops in Korea*

(Difficult, his forebears arrived in Texas ten years *after* the
massacre.)
It's tougher still on the way up.

> Under no circumstances will I ask for relief from
> this assignment in order to seek nomination to
> public office.
> *Dwight D. Eisenhower, commander of*
> *SHAPE, January 1952*

Two months later he did just that!

But public office has been that way for centuries. Henry VIII's trusted minister, Thomas Cromwell, waxed eloquent to his monarch about the new bride they had brought him, Anne of Cleves.

> Everyone praised her beauty, both of face and body, and one said she excelled the Duchess of Milan as the golden sun did the silver moon.

Henry's view was shared by the rest of the court.

> She is like a Flanders mare.

We all use white lies to convince us all is right in the world.

> The 300 Fabiae were not defeated: they were only killed.
>
> *Seneca*

> Q. How do you feel about being booed at your concert at Forest Hills?
> A. I thought it was great, I really did. If I said anything else I'd be a liar.
>
> *Bob Dylan*

> We are all moderates. The Labour Party is a moderate party.
>
> *Clive Jenkins, ASTMS general secretary*

> If you come up to the second floor of the White House, you'll see that it's just like anybody else's home.
>
> *Rosalynn Carter*

> We would not broadcast any programme if we thought it contained material that might be considered offensive.
>
> *BBC spokesman, after another deluge of complaints*

Though amongst all those histrionics and ballyhoo, sport surely boasts the superstars of the white lie.

Like Graham Gooch, leader of a rebel tour side to South Africa. He was getting £40 000 for a handful of matches, but claimed:

> We are only here to play cricket and follow our profession.

Not forgetting those who also serve, on the touchlines:

> There's only one United.
>> *British soccer chant. (There are 18 teams named 'United' in the English and Scottish football leagues)*

But who could top that 'magic' band of white liemongers, the managers and coaches.

> We murdered them, 0-0.
>> *Bill Shankly*

> There's a hell of a lot of politics in football. I don't think Henry Kissinger would have lasted 48 hours at Old Trafford.
>> *Tommy Docherty*

Docherty is the much-travelled soccer boss who, sacked (again) as manager of QPR, told the press:

> I still can't believe it.

Politicians vie with football managers for the honour of being the world's most consistent fibsters.

> If I ever should show any interest (*sic*) of yielding to persuasion please call in the psychiatrists, or even better, the sheriff. I feel that there can be no showing made that my duty extends beyond a one-term performance.
>> *Dwight D. Eisenhower, 1953. He went for a second term*

Could *The Real Paper*, Boston, have been telling the truth when, in 1975, they carried the ultimate political headline? The subject was the re-election campaign of Mayor Kevin White (he won). Simply, bluntly, in bold type they splashed:

WHITE LIES

7
FOR WHOM WE ARE ABOUT TO DECEIVE . . . .

'Any fool can tell the truth, but it requires a man of some sense to lie well,' wrote Samuel Butler. Well, to be reading this book proves you're a man – or woman – of some sense.

US Federal Employment expert George Kuper listed his three great lies of civilisation: 'The cheque is in the mail,' 'I'm going to love you as much in the morning as I do tonight.' And 'I'm from the Government, I'm here to help you.'

The real list is much, much longer, of course.

The lies	*Really meaning . . .*
POLITICS	
There is no alternative.	There are a great many alternatives.
The signs are positively encouraging.	Things are looking bleak.
We acknowledge there is a credibility gap.	We lied.
We agree in principle.	But we don't have the slightest intention of doing anything in practice.
The underlying trend is downwards.	If you can wait a couple of hundred years.
I think I have made myself perfectly clear.	I have been intentionally ambiguous.
We are not unduly concerned.	We are scared hollow.
Our relationship is the same as it has always been.	Daggers drawn.
There is a slight difference in emphasis.	In the way we're stabbing each other in the back.

I have no intention of resigning.	I expect to be fired.
I will be in my office first thing in the morning.	Clearing out my desk.
We never claimed it would be easy.	And if we did, more fool you lot for believing us.
There are still grounds for optimism.	If you believe in miracles.
Discussions were full, frank and business-like.	It was a hell of a row.
There is no disagreement.	It's all-out war.
The administration speaks with one voice.	It's just that it says twenty different things.
The effects will be minimal.	If you live in an igloo, and don't drink, smoke, pay tax, or eat.
Politics is about people.	Until they've voted.

BUSINESS LIES

He's in a meeting.	Please get off the line.
Can he call you back?	Will you stop bothering us.
It's good to hear from you.	It would be better still not to have done.
Sure I remember you.	Who the hell . . . ?
We must have lunch some-time.	Sometime, or better still, never.
Have I ever lied to you?	I always lie to you.
The product is meeting some consumer resistance.	Nobody will buy it.
The product is ahead of its time.	In ten years, still nobody will buy it.
The chairman is a very good friend of mine.	He once said hello to me in the lift.
You're the only person in the company who can do this job.	You're the only sucker who'll take it.

The chairman asked me to thank you personally.	No, you can't have a raise.
I'm doing this as a personal favour.	To myself.
Have I ever let you down?	Frequently.

OFFICIALDOM

It's a little administrative hiccup.	We've screwed it up badly.
It's a computer mal-function.	We've screwed it up totally.
Everybody's in the same boat, old man.	And we're up the creek without a paddle.
We're doing everything we can.	To push this on to someone else.
We can't work miracles.	And with the weekend coming up – no chance.
It's more than my job's worth.	If they paid me twice as much, I still wouldn't do it.
Somebody will be round first thing Monday.	Or the Monday after that, or the Tuesday after that, or the Wednesday . . . .
There's nothing to worry about. It's just a pre-caution.	So why should you care about dioxin/anthrax/gamma radiation. If you die, that's just more paperwork for us.

AT THE SHOPS

It ought to last a lifetime.	But it won't.
So very reasonable.	It's substandard.
It's a marvellous fit.	Though not on you.
They're fully waterproof.	As long as you don't get them wet.
You'll need this special aerosol.	Let's see what else we can do you for.

They're selling like hot cakes.

So, how many people have you seen buying hot cakes?

AT THE GARAGE

She's a little beauty.

But as to the car, it's a wreck.

Only 8000 miles.

On top of the 100 000 it did as a minicab.

One careful lady owner.

Before it became a mini-cab, hirecar, and was written off by a corn-flakes rep trying to race a Ferrari on the M4.

It'll be ready by 4.30.

We're just not saying which day.

It's not the parts, it's the labour you see.

It took us hours just to make up your bill.

I should buy a foreign car next time.

Then we'll be able to charge you even more.

That's it. You won't have any more trouble.

Until you try to put it in gear.

IN THE CAB

I've got nothing against ordinary drivers.

Just as long as they get out of my way.

I've got nothing against pedestrians.

I like having the chance to try to run them down.

What do you mean, one of those new £1 coins, you gave me 5p.

Got any more of those new £1 coins that look like 5p?

Not that I'm prejudiced.

Blacks, whites, browns, reds – I think they all should be shot.

And let's not forget that old favourite, the lie of omission:

Cuba's sugar production will go up 10 million tons a year!
Fidel Castro

But he didn't say when.

> Martial law is only a temporary solution. Most of
> the restrictions will be lifted by the end of the
> month.
>
> *Jozef Wiejacz, Polish deputy premier,*
> *February 1982*

He just didn't say which month.

Still the politicians try to deceive us, with so much, shall we say, bull . . . .

> The Soviet people wish the fraternal Polish people
> success in solving the difficult problems before their
> country, problems of historical importance for the
> destinies of the Polish state, to reliably ensure the
> further development of the Polish People's
> Republic along the path of socialism and peace.
>
> *Tass, after martial law was introduced*

How can you believe anyone who splits their infinitives?

> Not a bad start.
>
> *Jeremy Isaacs, head of Channel 4, on the*
> *station's disappointing opening*

> The results of our canvas have shown that the
> Labour vote has not only held up very well, but is
> increasing. I have myself been to 76 marginal
> constituencies and I have found a magnificent
> fighting spirit in the Labour Party, a belief that we
> can win and that we are going to win.
>
> *Michael Foot on his way to a drubbing,*
> *June 1983*

> Of course it's all been worthwhile.
>
> *Albert Spanswick, COHSE leader, on eight*
> *months of industrial action in pursuit of a*
> *12 per cent rise. Some of his members only*
> *got 6 per cent.*

47

I don't want to be leader of the party – I'm happy to be in the top dozen.

Margaret Thatcher, 1974

Labour would have won the election if we'd had more time to state our case.

Michael Foot, June 1983

All they needed was around five million more people to vote for them!

We have had a good measure of success. If we stick with it long enough I am confident that we will have reasonable success in achieving our objectives.

Ellsworth Bunker, US ambassador to Saigon, July 1967

Lewis Lehrman, after defeat for the Governorship of New York State, took things one stage further. He told party workers at his post-ballot oration:

We won.

A bit difficult to believe him.

Talking of what's difficult to believe, no anatomy of falsehood would be complete without a few words on advertising.

DR SCOTT'S ELECTRIC HAIRBRUSH
'An honest remedy. Recommended by the best physicians.'
Warranted to cure: Nervous Headache, Bilious Headache, Neuralgia – IN 5 MINUTES! Prevent falling hair and baldness! Cure dandruff and disease of the scalp! Promptly arrest premature greyness! Make the hair grow long and glossy! Immediately soothe the weary brain! 12s 6d post free from the proprietors.
Fraudulent imitations are utterly worthless.

1883 ad.

Just get that last line.

CARBOLIC SMOKE BALL WILL POSITIVELY CURE

Coughs. Cured in 1 week. Cold in the Head. Cured in 12 hours. Cold in the Chest. Cured in 12 hours. Bronchitis. Cured in every case. Influenza. Cured in 24 hours. Hay Fever. Cured in every case. Neuralgia. Cured in 10 minutes.

> *1892 ad. The Carbolic Smoke Ball Company were taken to court over it*

CONSUMPTION CAN BE CURED!

At last a remedy . . . that cures consumption . . . even in the advanced stages of the disease . . . after all other remedies have failed.

> *1900 ad.*

Ah, but things are different these days.

SOUTH AFRICA

'Scene of a dynamic development in race relations.'

> *Ad. in* Time *magazine*

Except for the occasional cure-all.

PRESIDENT MUSKIE – DON'T YOU FEEL BETTER ALREADY?

> *1972 bumper sticker*

Actually, no.

Sometimes we may even come to believe X washes whitest, after-shave Y will conjure up countless young ladies demanding to be ravaged, and that when Z came out for the first time it caused the whole population of Australia to riot, as they fought each other to spread it on their sandwiches.

But can we really believe those who say:

> Advertising is only reporting the facts.
> *John W. Hobson, US ad. director*

And:

Advertisements are the only truths to be relied on in a newspaper.

Thomas Jefferson

To use the ad-men's own buzz word, perhaps the 'ultimate' ad was this poster for the Advertising Standards Authority.

Are you legal, decent, honest and truthful?
Advertisers have to be.

Was this ad. truthful? Make up your own mind.

Mind you, advertisers aren't the only ones. There are statesmen:

I have fought all my life for independence. How can I leave now?

Joshua Nkomo, three days before fleeing Zimbabwe for exile in London

Mr Nkomo has no intention of returning to Zimbabwe for some months yet.

Spokesman for Joshua Nkomo, 36 hours before he flew back to Zimbabwe

There are policemen:

> Listen to the killer's voice. By phoning Leeds
> 464111 you can hear probably the most important
> clue to the killer's identity. His voice.
> > *West Yorkshire police ad. on the Yorkshire*
> > *Ripper. It wasn't him*

There are aristocrats:

> I don't think I've done anything to irritate.
> > *Unity Mitford, complaining of being*
> > *abused on a Fascist march, 1938*

Movie directors:

> I guess I'll just get on with my next movie and,
> who knows, fail gloriously.
> > *Steven Spielberg, after* Jaws *and* Close
> > Encounters

Presidents:

> I have full confidence in Anne Burford.
> > *Ronald Reagan, hours before she*
> > *'resigned' as head of the US environmental*
> > *protection agency*

And newspapermen:

> It is high time for the British public to be made
> aware of the fact that scandalous rumours about
> Princess Margaret are racing around the world.
> Newspapers in both Europe and America are
> openly asserting that the Princess is in love with a
> divorced man and that she wishes to marry him.
> Every newspaper which has printed the story names
> the man as Group Captain Peter Townsend. The
> story is of course utterly untrue.
> > The People, *June 1953*

8
IT'S A BOY!

'DEWEY DEFEATS TRUMAN' was the splash headline in the *Chicago Daily Tribune* on election night, 1948. Funny, I never remember much about President Dewey. 'It's going to be a boy!' proclaimed *The Sun* in its splash story shortly before the birth of the world's first test-tube baby – Louise Brown. Well, they nearly got it right.

Untruth will always out when people jump the gun.

> I think Jimmy's reign will revitalise the United States, as far as morals and everything else is concerned.
>
> *'Miz' Lillian Carter, 1976*

> Reagan could lose by a landslide.
>
> *Dr George Gallup, 1980*

> Just don't write him off, that's all. You fellows are due for a surprise tomorrow.
>
> *Barry Goldwater aides, eve of Presidential election, November 1964*

> We are absolutely on the edge of great television history.
>
> *David Frost, TV-am, January 1983*

> I don't rant and rave any more. I just put all my energies into playing better tennis.
>
> *Jimmy Connors, Wimbledon 1983, just before losing ignominiously to South African Kevin Curren, and storming out in a rage*

> Well, it looks like we've been badly licked.
>
> *President Woodrow Wilson to his secretary Joseph Tumulty, November 1916. Of course he went on to win*

It's no good, we shan't make it. I've checked with the slide rule. We've lost the election to Alec by one seat.

Harold Wilson, October 1964. They won

The following message was received as we were going to press:

New York, April 15
The Titanic sunk at 2.20 this morning. No lives were lost—Reuter

The Times, *16 April 1911*

HENRY KISSINGER: I don't see how the Democrats can recover from their electoral débâcle.
JOSEPH CALIFANO: Watergate will bring a Democratic revival.
HENRY KISSINGER: If that is what they are counting on they will be out of office for 30 years.

Conversation with former LBJ aide
reported in Kissinger's Years of Upheaval

By 1984 bigger and better stadiums will have been built to accommodate vaster and vaster crowds of football fans. Cinemas will have disappeared . . . . By 1984 gambling will have been nationalised and will be the greatest single source of revenue.

Sir Herbert Read, 1964

Tell that to the income tax man.

NOW IT'S 'ODDS ON' CHARLES TO WED DAVINA

I have reason to believe that in the luggage the Queen took with her to Polynesia last night was the announcement of Prince Charles's engagement to Davina Sheffield. According to my source the odds are 'four to one on' that she will release the news during her stay in Australia from March 4 to 8.

William Hickey, Daily Express, *February*
1977

I'm a born winner.
> *Ally McLeod, Scottish soccer boss, before Scotland's humiliating defeat in the 1978 World Cup*

THE WAR IN VIETNAM IS ENDED
> *Headline in* The Times, *January 1973*

FRANK CAPRA: You have made two movies, *Jaws* and *Close Encounters*, that should have climaxed your career. What are you going to do for an encore?
STEVEN SPIELBERG: I suppose make a dozen small failures.

COOLIDGE PROSPERITY IS PERMANENT
> *Republican slogan, 1927, before the Wall Street crash*

US presidential contests are known for spawning this kind of moonshine:

I'm gonna make him President.
> *Frank Sinatra on Spiro Agnew*

My First Days in the White House
> *Title of book published by the notorious and corrupt 'Kingfish', Governor and Senator Huey Long of Louisiana, 1935. He was assassinated the same year*

HUGHES ELECTED IN CLOSE CONTEST.
> *Headline in* The World, *1916. For later editions they did at least add a question mark*

The Spectator topped that in November 1980 when they declared Jimmy Carter elected for a second term.

CARTER'S WINNING STREAK
Henry Fairlie

Jimmy Carter will be the next President of the United States. The momentum is now with him and Ronald Reagan will not regain it . . . .

It wouldn't have been so bad if the author had not added:

I'm not just making a guess. I am reinforcing my political judgments of the past months.

Yahboo his political judgments, then!

TORIES NEED A MIRACLE NOW
Splash headline in The Observer, *June 1970*

The British General Election of 1970 was a classic – defying pollsters, pundits and politicians alike.

Short of a miraculous turn-around in public opinion, Mr Wilson is headed straight back to Downing Street, probably with an increased majority.
Ronald Butt, Sunday Times, *14 June 1970*

TODAY'S POLL VERDICT: 100-SEAT MAJORITY FOR WILSON?
Headline, The Observer, *14 June 1970*

What will become of the Tories after a third successive poll defeat?
Peter Jenkins, The Guardian, *15 June 1970*

You'd have thought they'd have got it right by the next British General Election in February 1974. But no.

The present one-sided picture of a relaxed and 'statesmanlike' Prime Minister chastising the militants on behalf of the nation and a rather tired and rattled Labour leader swinging wildly, can only produce one result.
David Watt, Financial Times, *February 1974*

Victory to the rattled Labour leader, swinging wildly. Why must people jump the gun?

> In 1984, there isn't a petrol gauge on your dashboard, just a tiny bulb which will light up to warn you that the fuel cell which powers your car needs attention. And that bulb hasn't lit up for nearly a year now . . . . Remote control rockets hurtle overhead loaded with mail and light cargoes. Higher still will streak great airlines which can cross from London to New York in 90 minutes. You race over a canal bridge, waving to your neighbour at the wheel of his hovercraft . . . .
>
> *Ronald Brech, statistician, 1963*

> In 1984, Parliament will be televised . . . most of the political restrictions now imposed on newspapers but not television will be abolished . . . the important device of television-plus-telephone will make the farthest journey seem unnecessary.
>
> *Sir Gerald Barry, 1964*

Not *quite* right.

> ANNIHILATION OF SOVIET ARMIES ALMOST CONCLUDED
>
> Völkischer Beobachter, *German newspaper, 1941*

> I have no bitterness against that man Smith. But one day he will hand over everything to me.
>
> *Joshua Nkomo*

He handed over everything to Robert Mugabe.

> Obviously, the American economy today is not in a depression; indeed, the 1980 recession, which began in January, almost certainly ended in the third quarter.
>
> *Leonard Silk,* New York Times, *1981, when America was gripped by recession*

Oh no it didn't.

> If I wasn't here, I'd probably be drinking with Judy Garland now.
>
> *Ronnie Kray, gangster, in the dock at the Old Bailey, March 1969*

> I would only give myself an outside chance.
>
> *Shirley Williams, on her prospects at the Crosby by-election*

> I am not losing this election, I am winning it.
>
> *John Butcher, Tory candidate at Crosby*

As Bismarck said, people never lie so much as after a hunt, during a war – and before an election.

> Social Democrat founder Roy Jenkins is facing a disastrous defeat at the Glasgow Hillhead by-election.
>
> *Splash story in the* Sunday Mirror *by Victor Knight, March 1982*

> I am not faltering. I am confident of winning.
>
> *Peter Tatchell at Bermondsey, February 1983*

Despite a disastrous start to his campaign, the Labour candidate, Mr Peter Tatchell, goes into the second week of the Bermondsey by-election with every reason to believe he will win. He is still on course to take a comfortable majority of votes in this South London constituency.

> *Martin Linton,* The Guardian, *February 1983*

DARLINGTON LABOUR VOTE IS CRUMBLING
Defeat is not far off for Labour . . . the party has a slim chance of victory on 24 March . . .

> The Observer, *March 1983*

It feels good, it feels right.

> *Michael Fallon, Tory candidate at the*
> *Darlington by-election (needless to say,*
> *Labour won)*

On the subject of winners:

I'm a winner.

> *Allan Clarke. February 1982, before taking*
> *Leeds United into the Second Division and*
> *being fired*

We have the better talent. David Frost is the most successful and gifted presenter in the world today. Anna Ford is the most beautiful woman in England. Ours is the better team. It can't fail.

> *Peter Jay, TV-am, March 1983*

Foinavon: He can be safely ignored even in a race noted for shocks.

> *National newspaper tipster, Grand*
> *National, April 1967. Foinavon won*

I have never resigned from any job.

> *Ally McLeod, Scottish soccer manager,*
> *after disaster in the World Cup, June 1978.*
> *Three months later he resigned to join Ayr*
> *United*

I don't play golf. That's a cissy game. Who wants to play golf?

> *Arnold Palmer, 15, when his father tried*
> *to get him on to the fairway*

It's impossible. You're too short and your voice is too high-pitched.

> *Richard Burton's father on his son's plans*
> *to be an actor*

Tell her that in America men don't like fat women.

> *Louis B. Mayer to Greta Garbo's agent*

Let us finally consider the lot of the poor critics. After the sinking of HMS Sheffield during the Falklands war, a TV special on Horatio Nelson due to be shown that night provoked a bitter row. Television critic Nancy Banks-Smith wrote in *The Guardian* the next day:

> Never have I known a programme so apt and so unfortunate in its timing.

That's what comes of jumping the gun. The programme was never shown!

9
TWENTY-FIVE LIES TO FLOOR A DOORSTEP CALLER

1 That's the phone ringing, it's Australia.

2 I can definitely smell burning.

3 Actually my brother owns a double glazing firm (when he's not being a Lloyd's underwriter, painter and decorator, encyclopaedia salesman, and making his own plastic brushes).

4 I'll see you in a fortnight (if you can find me in Marbella).

5 I know No 24 are *very interested* – if you rush round there right now you just might catch them.

6 I'm hopeless without my glasses – I can only read the small print.

7 My husband will be back in two minutes – he's a policeman.

8 I'm so glad you called, we're looking for some generous people for Sally's sponsored swim.

9 Come and look at our holiday slides first, then we'll talk about it later.

10 Everyone's got double glazing these days. Can't you do quadruple?

11 Of course I'll vote for you – but you'll have to bribe me more than the Labour candidate.

12 My husband's just had a hernia. Are you any good at moving grand pianos?

13 Are you any good at unblocking drains?

14 Would you like to meet our pet anaconda?

15 We're all nudists here. You'll have to take your clothes off there on the step.

16 A shame about the last encyclopaedia man, wasn't it? Nasty business.

17 We'd love to help, but we're all down with typhoid.

18 Try not to breathe in. We're just stripping down all the blue asbestos in the hall.

19 I'm so glad you've called. Could you look at the dog for me? I think it's got rabies.

20 Could you help me feed the Piranha fish?

21 It's all right, my husband's just playing with his chemistry set. It's just that some people are scared of gamma radiation.

22 Actually we're all cannibals. Why not come in and have a bacon sandwich?

23 Have you ever been to a ritual sacrifice?

24 I suppose you've heard of AIDS. Well . . . .

25 Can you just wait a minute? My husband's in the kitchen cleaning his sawn-off shotgun.

10
WHITEWASH AT THE WHITE HOUSE

'I don't make jokes – I just watch the government and report the facts,' said Will Rogers. Irving F. Stone put it more bluntly: 'Every government is run by liars and nothing they say should be believed.'

Jokers or liars? The record of Presidents of the United States for telling the truth is a little better than that. Perhaps George Washington and the apple tree ('I cannot tell a lie. I did it with my little hatchet') set the tone.

There have been notable exceptions. You can imagine a young man from Whittier, California, handling the apple tree scam a little differently. He went on to be President, of course, at a time of sweetness and light:

> I reject the cynical view that politics is inevitably, or even usually, a dirty business.
> > *Richard Nixon, August 1973*

> I want there to be no question remaining that the President has nothing to hide in this matter.
> > *Handing over the White House tapes on TV, April 1974. (This was the lie that finished him.)*

US presidents were always prone to bluff.

> There is every reason to believe that our system will soon attain the highest degree of perfection of which human institutions are capable.
> > *James Monroe, 1820*

Hadn't he thought of Nixon?

> This desk of mine is one at which a man may die, but from which he cannot resign.
> > *Dwight D. Eisenhower*

Hadn't he thought of Nixon?

The White House is the finest jail in the world.

Harry S. Truman

He had thought about Nixon.

Whitewash at the White House was not the personal innovation of that young man from Whittier, however. As far back as 1874 President Ulysses S. Grant declared, on the exposure of the St Louis whiskey ring:

Let no guilty man escape.

Then made sure his secretary, a man named Babcock, did just that.

Of course, some would later argue:

When the President does it, that means that it is not illegal.

Richard Nixon, May 1977

Well, not quite. But more than one President has been found to be . . . er . . . not exactly telling the truth.

I have told you once and I have told you again – your boys will not be sent into any foreign wars.

Franklin D. Roosevelt, 1940

An officer fit for duty who at this crisis would abandon his post to electioneer . . . ought to be scalped.

Rutherford Hayes, 1874. It didn't stop him campaigning and being elected to Congress

The great object of my administration will be to arrest . . . the agitation of the slavery question and to destroy sectional parties.

James Buchanan, 1857

And on to the civil war.

If you want WAR vote for HUGHES
If you want Peace and honour

63

VOTE FOR WILSON
And continued prosperity.

Election ad., 1916

They voted for Wilson (narrowly) and got war just the same.

> Our first object must be to provide security from poverty and want . . . . We want to see a nation built of home owners and farm owners. We want to see their savings protected. We want to see them in steady jobs. We want them all secure.
>
> *Herbert Hoover, inaugural address, 1928*

And on to the Wall Street crash.

> The United States must be neutral in fact as well as in name during these days that are to try men's souls.
>
> *Woodrow Wilson, 1914*

And so on to the First World War.

> America's present need is not heroics, but healing; not nostrums but normalcy; not revolution, but restoration; not surgery, but serenity.
>
> *Warren Harding, 1921*

And on to the Teapot Dome affair, when an oil corruption scandal rocked the presidency.

> I hope the United States will keep out of this war. I believe that it will.
>
> *Franklin D. Roosevelt, fireside radio chat, September 1939*

It didn't, of course. Mind you, FDR's famous New Deal, running up deficits to finance a vast public works programme and a massive jobs expansion, must have come as a shock to many of his supporters. He came to power on a pledge to balance the budget!

In the strongest language you can command you
may say that I have no political ambitions at all.
Make it even stronger than that if you wish.

> *Dwight D. Eisenhower, 1945*

American presidents have been known to say astonishing
things from time to time.

The freedom of the press is one of the most
zealously guarded aspects of our national heritage.

> *Richard Nixon, 1973*

I do not genuinely believe that there is any single
person anywhere in the world who wants peace as
much as I want it.

> *Lyndon B. Johnson, 1968*

The great, generous Russian people have been
added in all their naive majesty and might to the
forces that are fighting for freedom in the world,
for justice and peace.

> *Woodrow Wilson, 1917*

I would have made a good Pope.

> *Richard Nixon*

No matter what anyone said I knew that the people
out there loved me a great deal. All that talk about
my lack of charisma is a lot of crap. After all that
I'd done for them and I'd given them, how could
they help but love me?

> *Lyndon B. Johnson*

Mind you, he did once say:

A nation that knows how to popularise
commodities ranging from cornflakes to luxury
automobiles certainly should be able to tell the rest
of the world the truth about what it is doing and
why.

> *Lyndon B. Johnson, June 1961*

Which made it a pity, when he came to office, that he pledged:

> We are going to build a Great Society – where no man is the victim of fear or poverty or hatred, where every man has a chance for fulfilment, prosperity, and hope.

It got worse later on.

> We will not be defeated. We will not grow tired. We will not withdraw, either openly or under the cloak of a meaningless agreement.
> > *On Vietnam, April 1965*

LBJ was not the only US President with a penchant for speaking 'famous last words'.

> The ballot is stronger than the bullet.
> > *Abraham Lincoln, 1856*

> I suppose they know what they're doing.
> > *Warren Harding, signing an order for the transfer of oil rights from Elk Hills and Teapot Dome to the Department of the Interior. A corrupt official of the Department was later convicted of leasing them out in return for a hefty bribe.*

> I have no ambitions to hold office after July 1977.
> > *Gerald Ford, to Richard Nixon, 1973*

Just as well he lost the 1976 Presidential election, then.

> The fundamental business of this country is on a sound and prosperous basis.
> > *Herbert Hoover, 1929, just before the Wall Street crash*

> Make no mistake about it – we are going to win.
> > *Lyndon B. Johnson on Vietnam, 1968*

NIXON: Haldeman and Erlichman are guilty until we have evidence.

NEWSMAN: Mr President, I think you made a slip there.

NIXON: Yes, I certainly did . . . thank you for correcting me.

> *Richard Nixon, press conference,*
> *November 1973*

As Jerry Ford said:

I guess it just proves that anyone can be President.

Ronald Reagan went even further:

You can believe me. I'm not smart enough to lie.

11
OVER MY DEAD BODY

'Britain was the richest country in the world until the
politicians got at it,' said California's anti-tax law
campaigner, Howard Jarvis. 'There is a vast amount of
humbug in the House of Commons,' said Arthur Hopkinson
MP. 'But it really does very little harm, because we all know
it's humbug.'

Certainly if you wish to see professional fibsters in action,
there's nowhere to beat the ancient Palace of Westminster.

The joke is that the MPs there swear, shout and even fight
with each other. But no member may accuse another of lying.
They must realise it would take up too much of their time.

Winston Churchill got round the ban by using phrases like
'terminological inexactitude'. And there have certainly been a
few of those over the years.

Perhaps the worst period was the 1960s and 1970s. Every
election, the politicians promised the earth. But all they left
was fertile ground for those who believe – like John
Arbuthnot – 'All political parties die at last of swallowing
their own lies.'

Just hear them talk:

> It will not be enough for a Conservative
> Government to make a fresh start with new
> policies . . . . We must create a new way of running
> our national affairs . . . it means dealing honestly
> and openly with the House of Commons, with the
> press and with the public.
>
> *Edward Heath, Foreword to 1970*
> *Conservative Manifesto 'A Better*
> *Tomorrow'*

He went on, of course, to preside over the most secretive and
un-open government since the war.

But what about Labour?

> Being genuine, plain-speaking men, they find it
> extremely difficult to tell lies well.
>
> The Diplomatist *magazine, 1968*

What a hoot! And that right in the middle of the premiership of Harold Wilson – the Sir John Barbirolli of political doubletalk:

> That does not mean, of course, that the pound here in Britain, in your pocket or purse, or in your bank, has been devalued.
>
> *Harold Wilson, on the devaluation of the pound, 1967*

Or more seriously:

> The facilities for further borrowing which have been . . . . built up these past few years have given us a firm base from which we can advance without panic measures, without devaluation, without stop and go measures.
>
> *Harold Wilson, October 1964*

He gave Britain them all.

> As to the idea of freezing all wage claims, salary claims . . . . I think this would be monstrously unfair . . . . I do not think you could ever legislate for wage increases, and no party is setting out to do that.
>
> *Harold Wilson, March 1966*

He announced legislation for a wage freeze four months later.

> We intend to play the ball and not the man . . . .
>
> *Harold Wilson on Sir Alec Douglas-Home, 1963*

He played the man.

> HAROLD WILSON TELLS TSR2 WORKERS: 'YOUR JOBS ARE SAFE UNDER LABOUR. LABOUR WILL NOT CANCEL THE TSR2'
>
> *1964 election leaflet to aero workers*

They cancelled the TSR2.

> Q. Will the grammar schools be abolished?
> A. Over my dead body.
>
> *Harold Wilson, May 1963*

They abolished the grammar schools.

The TV satire show *That Was The Week That Was* skitted:
Q. How do you tell when Harold Wilson's lying? A. When his lips are moving.

Unfortunately, Mr Wilson's rival, Ted Heath, caught the same bug.

> Once a decision is made, once a policy is established, the Prime Minister and his colleagues should have the courage to stick with it.
>
> *Foreword to 'A Better Tomorrow', 1970*

All very well, except that the very same manifesto pledged:

> We utterly reject the philosophy of compulsory wage control.

'Laughing Ted' fought the next election on the issue of statutory wage control – and lost!

> There will be no further large-scale immigration.

Then came the Ugandan Asians.

> We are totally opposed to further nationalisation of British industry.

Then they nationalised Rolls Royce.

> This would, at a stroke, reduce the rise in prices, increase productivity and reduce unemployment.
>
> *1970 election leaflet*

Oh dear. Inflation went up to record levels during Mr Heath's government.

Of course, the Wilson-Heath broken promises so turned off

the public from politicians, they have tended to tread just a little more warily since.

Though not the SDP.

The new party's leaders were all ministers under Wilson. They obviously felt nostalgic for the style.

> I would not join a centre party because I feel the whole idea is wrong.
>
> *Shirley Williams, 1980*

> There is a lot of talk about a centre party – and that I might lead it. I find this idea profoundly unattractive.
>
> *Roy Jenkins, 1973*

The watershed in political honesty had been the British devaluation crisis of November 1967:

> The Labour Party gives defence of the pound the first priority. We shall need to sacrifice all other considerations to make sterling strong.
>
> *Harold Wilson, February 1958*

> Devaluation would be regarded all over the world as an acknowledgement of defeat, a recognition that we were not on a springboard, but a slide.
>
> *Harold Wilson, July 1961*

But of course this was not the only 'bull' of the Wilson years.

> I see no need for a Royal Commission [on trade unions] which will take minutes and waste years.
>
> *Harold Wilson, September 1964*

Within six months he'd announced one.

> The Industrial Relations Bill is an essential Bill – essential to our economic recovery, essential to the balance of payments, essential to full employment.
>
> The passage of this Bill is essential to the

Government's continuance in office. There is no going back on that.

Harold Wilson, April 1969

You didn't believe him, did you? Two months later, after ferocious trade union opposition, the project was scrapped.
  The Wilson example was, like we said, contagious.

We have no intention of ratting on any of our commitments. We intend to remain and still remain fully capable of carrying out all the commitments we have at the present time, including the Far East, the Middle East and Africa. We do intend to remain in every sense a world power.

Denis Healey, 1966

Within two years, it was announced Britain was withdrawing from the Persian Gulf and the whole of the Far East, except Hong Kong.

My colleagues and I will never use words or support actions which exploit or intensify divisions in our society.

Edward Heath, June 1970

Tell that to the miners.

I have set and always will set my face like flint against making any difference between one citizen of this country and another on the grounds of his origin.

Enoch Powell, October 1964

I would sum up the period 1966 to 1970 by putting it this way: 1966 will be the year of attack; 1967 will be the year of advance; 1968-70 will be the years of achievement.

James Callaghan, 1966

Well, why do you think they called him 'Sunny Jim'?
  The economy has always been top of the government 'lie league'.

With the Conservatives prices are steadier.
> *Conservative campaign guide, 1970*

We are top of the league in the fight against inflation.
> *Harold Wilson, October 1974*

He meant, of course, that by 1975 Britain would be top of the West European league table of inflation itself!

I have cut the inflation rate I inherited by half.
> *Denis Healey, Chancellor of the Exchequer, September 1974*

He meant that by the following June, he'd have doubled it.

The battle against inflation is won. And I'm bringing back a certificate from Washington to prove it.
> *Denis Healey, October 1977*

Peace in our time.
  But a little bit of bluster and bluff does add colour to politics, doesn't it. Not to mention the odd wholesale U-turn.

We should not have any further defence cuts if the realm is to be properly and effectively defended.
> *Margaret Thatcher, January 1976*

The defence of Britain is only one of three areas of public expenditure which, under a Conservative government, would be exempt from further cuts.
> *Sir Geoffrey Howe, 1976*

As we've said, on to the Falklands. Though recently, it's not just been the Tories:

What is needed is a socialist philosophy outside the restrictive confines of much of the present polarised political debate.
> *David Owen,* Face the Future, *hardback edition (before founding of the SDP), 1981*

What is needed is a *political* philosophy outside the restrictive confines of much of the present polarised political debate.

> *David Owen,* Face the Future, *paperback edition (after founding of the SDP), 1981*

My italics!

The challenge *to British socialism* is not to allow this political critique to be mounted only from the standpoint of the Right, but to ensure that *the Left* is also heard to be reassessing the strength of the corporate state with conviction and coherence.

> *David Owen,* Face the Future, *hardback edition*

The challenge *for social democrats* is not to allow this political critique to be mounted only from the viewpoint of the Right, but to ensure that *the Social Democratic Party* is seen to be reassessing the strength of the corporate state with conviction and coherence.

> *David Owen,* Face the Future, *paperback edition*

Despite her denials, the lady has been caught a-U-turning herself. In June 1981, when unemployment was 2.3 million, Mrs Thatcher said:

There are now clear signs the worst of the recession is over.

The jobless total rose another million.

Before the 1979 election, she said:

Taxes must and taxes will come down.

In the next four years, taxes for the average family didn't come down – they went up £5 a week.

On 18 April 1979, Mrs Thatcher said:

We have no intention to raise National Health prescription charges.

Her Government raised them from 20p to £1.40 – a 600 per cent increase.

Finally, how's this for a laugh:

> There are a lot of potential Freddie Lakers waiting to do their stuff for themselves and the country. A Tory government will give them the encouragement they need.
>
> *Sir Keith Joseph, Conservative industry spokesman, 1977*

12
LIE FOLLOWS BY POST

'There is no waste of time in life like that of making explanations,' said Benjamin Disraeli. And as Prime Minister and the leading politician of his day, he must have had to make plenty. 'The most awful thing one can do is to tell the truth,' said George Bernard Shaw. 'It's all right in my case because I'm not taken seriously.'

For those who *are* serious enough to want to know the difference between a diplomatic illness and pneumonia, here's a plain man's guide to excuses. Escape clauses. Get-outs.

After all, few are as honest as Lord Charles Beresford, who replied to an invitation: 'Very sorry, can't come. Lie follows by post.'

Weasel words	*Meaning*
POLITICAL GET-OUTS	
It's a question of priorities.	And our priority right now is not to do it.
It's international interest rates/the world recession/the rise/fall in OPEC quotas.	We're trying our best to blame someone else.
It's a purely seasonal phenomenon.	That happens spring, winter, summer, autumn . . . .
The Government were forced to take this unusual step.	Because we messed it up.
We inherited this problem from the previous Administration.	We just made it ten times worse.
Few people are likely to be affected.	Everyone will be affected.
I've been quoted out of context.	I wish I'd never said it.

I was speaking off the record.

I definitely wish I'd never said it.

This would not be appropriate at the present time.

We don't want to do it.

It would be extremely difficult to legislate at the present time.

It would be extremely easy to legislate at the present time.

We are examining all the possibilities.

To wheedle our way out of it.

Measures will be enacted within the lifetime of the next Government.

We're putting it off for ever.

BUSINESS EXCUSES

It's in the post.

Or might be one day.

It's circumstances beyond our control.

We can't help being incompetent.

These things take time.

Especially when you're incompetent.

I know it's here somewhere.

I've definitely lost it.

I've got a very important lunch date.

With a very pretty blonde from downstairs.

We're having a small problem with the workforce.

They're on strike.

It'll be all straightened out in a day or two.

It'll be all straightened out in a year or two.

I've no idea how it got through quality control.

Except that we don't have a quality control.

ME – DISHONEST?

It fell off the back of a lorry.

It's stolen.

It's one of the perks of the job.

As long as the cops don't catch you.

Everyone is doing it.	I thought I'd get away with it.
Jim said it would be OK.	Jim said I'd get away with it.
Nobody's worried these days.	Doesn't everyone get away with it?
I've never done this before.	And been caught.
The payments have not affected my judgment or decision-making in any way.	Just my bank balance.
I was overcome by a strange sensation.	I decided to become a crook.
It's totally out of character.	I thought I was Al Capone.
I don't know what came over me.	Sheer naked greed.
It can only be those hay fever pills.	Let's see if the judge will swallow this one.
God told me to do it.	If he'd only made me rich, all this wouldn't have happened in the first place.

REFUSING AN INVITE

We've got something else on . . .	From about five seconds ago.
. . . a terrible cold	Don't want to come.
. . . flu.	Definitely don't want to come.
Guwoo goo joo.	I've just had all my teeth out.
What a shame! That's the night we go to the supermarket.	What luck! That's the night we go to the supermarket.
The car's broken down.	It's too far to travel.
The car's been in a smash.	It's definitely too far to travel.

His boss is coming that
   night – it's the only night
   he can come round.

Unless you offer us
   another date, in which
   case he can come then.

We can't get a baby sitter.

We want to watch
   Dynasty.

We can't get a granny
   sitter.

We want to watch *Minder*.

Gloria's broken her leg.

She's been at the
   Dubonnet.

Gloria's broken both legs.

She's been at the gin.

We've got Aunt Esme
   from Huddersfield.

We're going to the theatre.

We've got Uncle Jack
   from Catford.

We're going to the dogs.

We're expecting a call
   from Chippewa Falls,
   Wisconsin.

Tonight, the next night,
   and every night.

It's my parents' golden
   wedding.

We celebrate it every
   Friday night.

ON BEING LATE

I didn't realise the time.

It's easy when you don't
   look at your watch.

My car broke down again.

Funny how it breaks down
   eight times a week.

My watch stopped.

Funny how it stops twelve
   times a week.

I couldn't get away.

From the bar.

I ran into Frank – you
   know Frank –

Yes, he's in Saudi Arabia.

AT THE SHOPS

It's out of guarantee *or*
   You've tampered with it.

Your money back? We'll
   soon get out of this one.

It must be you. I can't
   see/hear/smell anything.

Your money back? We'll
   definitely get out of this
   one.

You've worn these shoes in the rain.

Just because they're waterproof doesn't mean to say you can get them wet.

No one has ever complained before.
What do you expect at that price?

Not in the last half-hour anyway.
Shoddy workmanship.

FEMALE EXCUSES

I've got a headache.
I've got to wash my hair.
It was an absolute bargain.

I don't want to do it.
I still don't want to do it.
If your name's Rockefeller.

MALE EXCUSES

I told him to stick his rotten job.
I didn't see the red light.

I've been fired.

I was too busy watching out for police patrols.

The referee was against us.
It's the male menopause.

We played like lemons.
Touché! That's my answer to your headache.

And still the weasel words, brash, brazen, inventive, go on:

My assassination attempt was an act of love.
John Hinckley Jnr

Every people has the right to get rid of their enemies.
Col. Muammar Gaddafi, defending his foreign 'hit squads'

You'd better watch out, then.

The music speaks to you every day. It says rise. It says kill. Why blame it on me? I didn't write the music.
Charles Manson

I heard voices from God. It was important to my cause. I had to carry on with the mission.

> *Peter Sutcliffe, 'The Yorkshire Ripper'*

I was only inspired to *shoot* the President. The doctors finished the work. It is the Deity's act, not mine.

> *Charles Julius Guiteau, who shot President Garfield, 1881*

I don't think people mind a little downright rudeness or prejudice.

> *Prince Philip*

In *The Mummy* I only kill three people – and not in a ghastly way. I just break their necks.

> *Christopher Lee*

What is the difference between killing people with stones and killing people with bullets? But throwing stones certainly teaches people a lesson.

> *Ayatollah Khalkhali, Iran's 'Judge Blood'*

We apologise to our readers for any delay in the delivery of this week's paper, which is due to industrial action forced on the rail unions by the British Rail board and the Tory government.

> Tribune, *April 1972*

Off the record . . .

I thought I was giving an interview for background purposes only and was going to be given a final draft. I would never have let it go forward . . . .

> *Mgr Bruce Kent, after interview with* Woman *magazine lambasting the Pope*

I am not a buffoon, a boob or a wacko, as some public figures have so described me. I am a common citizen with uncommon financial and family problems.

> *Billy Carter*

And still the weasel words . . . . A driving instructor from Crewe (yes – Crewe), fined £50 for indecent assault on a woman learner, told the court:

> Very occasionally it is necessary for the instructor to regulate the pupil's clutch pressure. Some instructors give a shout, but I prefer a light touch to the upper leg.

After a raid on a Los Angeles 'auction' police bought a man for $16 dollars and then prosecuted what they called 'sado-masochistic homosexuals' under an old slavery statute. Gay leaders protested:

> This was not a slave market. It was a fund-raising event for a VD clinic.

More celebrated was the case of suburban madam Mrs Cynthia Payne, made famous by the house slogan: 'We also accept luncheon vouchers.' After the police raided Mrs Payne's establishment and rounded up the customers, one 70-year-old gentleman excused himself with the memorable line:

> I'm a bit past it. I'm only here because it's a Christmas party.

Another one compromised was Martin Preedy, a naval rating fined £100 by Newcastle magistrates for streaking. His commanding officer told the court:

> He is a lively extrovert, the sort who would win a VC.

Just one question. Where would they pin it?
Some more crazy defences:

> I decided to make bombs when I became dissatisfied with the Young Conservatives.
> *Robert Trigg, British student terrorist*

Arrested for housebreaking, Chicago salesman Dennis McKerron admitted 200 robberies, netting a total of £35 000. He said:

> I needed the money to pay my lawyers to get me off a fraud charge.

Kevin White, the Mayor of Boston, excused himself for paying his wife 19 000 dollars out of campaign funds by saying:

> She said she was worth 50 000 dollars, but I couldn't afford that.

And finally Richard Twinn, 39, accused of criminal damage at his ex-girlfriend's house, blamed it all on time-travel through the galaxy, courtesy of a well-known BBC-TV sci-fi show:

> I thought I was Dr Who. An inner force drove me to her home. After waiting around the corner for some time I saw a telephone booth. I walked in and thought it was a spaceship or time machine. When I came out, I checked the date on my watch. It showed the year 1991. The illusion was further enhanced by a jet flying overhead with its red and green landing lights flashing.

The judge was unimpressed. For his close encounter with the law, Mr Twinn was fined £150. Also refused: his request for a million years to pay.

13
THE ROYAL PREROGATIVE

'Perhaps the thing I might do best is to be a long distance lorry driver,' said Princess Anne. 'I'd swap with you any time,' Princess Diana told humble Australian housewife Jill Shoebridge during a walkabout in Canberra.

Fibbing isn't confined to mere commoners.

You could say it's the Royal prerogative. As budding Royal Lieut. Mark Phillips said on rumours he was to be engaged to Princess Anne:

> It's absolute nonsense. There is no truth in it whatsoever.
>
> *Mark Phillips, December 1972*

His feelings were Royally reciprocated.

> There is no romance between us, and there are no grounds for rumours of a romance between us.
>
> *Princess Anne, March 1973*

> If Princess Anne has said this herself, perhaps Fleet Street will now believe her and let the Princess and Lieutenant Phillips train their horses alone in peace.
>
> *Buckingham Palace spokesman, March 1973*

In fact, right up to 28 May 1973 the Palace were saying about rumours of an engagement:

> These stories are in the realm of speculation.

You guessed. The engagement of HRH Princess Anne and Captain Mark Phillips was announced just *one day later*, on May 29.

But the press office at Buckingham Palace have been known for – well, the odd dubious proclamation.

After a 'near-miss' between a Miami-bound 747 and a plane described as a 'Royal or rogue flight' in November 1981, the Palace pronounced:

No members of the Royal family were flying in the vicinity.

No members of the Royal Family *were* flying in the vicinity. Just one – Prince Philip. He was at the controls of the RAF Andover involved in the near miss. It was later revealed that the plane was at the wrong altitude.

More recently there was the Koo Stark affair. When there was something of a furore about Prince Andrew taking the young former starlet on holiday to Mustique, Buckingham Palace declared:

> There is no question of the Prince's holiday being cut short. He is definitely not coming back tomorrow as has been reported.

Later that same day:

> We are not now denying the Prince is returning home tomorrow. There will be no one else with him.

In March 1983, there was a similar charade over Prince Andrew's bodyguard, Detective Inspector Steve Burgess. He flew home early from the Caribbean after a rumoured row that had begun when he banned one of Prince Andrew's girlfriends from a party.

Said the Palace:

> There is no question of Mr Burgess being replaced for any other reason than normal turn around of duty.

Within 24 hours they'd changed their mind.

> This is what we said last night. We have now changed our position.

But, let's face it. The Royals are a little above – well, *most* of the rest.

85

What a pity. Britain is losing its two most eligible bachelors in a year – David and Prince Charles.

Lynne Frederick, on becoming engaged to
David Frost

I'm, along with the Queen, y'know, one of the best things England's got – me and the Queen.

Mick Jagger

That's not to say that the Royals themselves haven't been known to – well, bend the truth a bit.

All the Royals are very frugal. If someone extra turns up for lunch on Sunday, it's very difficult to find another portion of food.

Stephen Barry, former valet to Prince
Charles

We've never had a holiday. A week or ten days at Balmoral or Sandringham is the nearest we get.

Princess Anne

Dog leads cost money.
> *The Queen to young Prince Charles*

This isn't ours. It's just a tied cottage.
> *Prince Philip on Buckingham Palace*

We've had to sell a small yacht and I shall have to give up polo soon, things like that.
> *Prince Philip pleading poverty on American TV, 1970*

Surely not. Though in his student days, Charles turned down a selection of ties in a shop in Cambridge saying:

Too expensive.

At Gordonstoun during a pottery lesson, Prince Andrew ticked off a prankster who stole his apron to use as a towel with the words:

Hey, cut that out. Laundering things costs money.

Said Princess Anne:

There is no question of just going out and buying a horse. I don't have the sort of money available that you need to buy a top horse at the present time.

Princess Anne is as aware of our financial position as I am and we decided we would have to cut back, or find money from sponsorship. We are a young couple with a mortgage.
> *Capt. Mark Phillips*

But Palace life still seems romantic.

I have been wounded by the dart of love.
> *Henry VIII, love letter to Anne Boleyn*

Trouble was, his axe was sharper.

The English have been so kind and lovely.
Mrs Wallis Simpson, December 1935

Well, to her face, perhaps.

I am determined to follow in my father's footsteps and to work as he did through his life for the happiness and welfare of his subjects.
Edward VIII, 1936

He kept telling me he was a confirmed bachelor and I thought, at least one knows where one stands.
Princess Anne on Capt. Mark Phillips

But does he know where *he* stands?

I'm just there to make up the numbers.
Capt. Mark Phillips

It could be worse.

Give thanks to God with us for the good life we are leading and hope to lead with our present Queen . . . after sundry troubles of mind which have happened to us by marriages.
Henry VIII on Catherine Howard

Twelve weeks later he had her executed.

I sent for the Prime Minister and gave him a piece of my mind. I told the cheeky so-and-so that I would abdicate if he made war. There was a frightful scene. But you needn't worry. There won't be a war.
Edward VIII to German ambassador Von Hoesch, 1936

And *after* the war?

I've no definite plans for setting up a permanent home in England. But there's no reason why I should not.
Duke of Windsor, 1945

Oh no?

The British Royal Family are the most popular and revered in the world. But one sometimes does wonder . . . should one be *a little* sceptical . . . ?

> I'm delighted to see Joey Gormley and I'm delighted he calls me Charlie.
>
> *Prince Charles*

> I feel positively delighted and frankly amazed that Diana is prepared to take me on.
>
> *Prince Charles on his engagement*

> The first thing I want is a pint of milk.
>
> *Unlikely request from Prince Andrew, returning from 5½ months in the Falklands*

> I wish I'd worn my jeans.
>
> *Prince Charles at Status Quo rock concert*

14
NO ONE CAN EXIST ON
HALF A MILLION A YEAR . . .

'Young people, nowadays, imagine money is everything,' said
Oscar Wilde. 'And when they grow older they know it.' The
problem is, as we all know, life is so expensive.

As Lord Butler of Saffron Walden put it: 'Half a million
doesn't go far nowadays.' Or, hark at international multi-
millionaire financier Sir James Goldsmith: 'Any wise person
keeps 600 million dollars cash handy for a good deal.'

Money may not be the root of all evil. But it is certainly the
root of much deception. More lies are told about that lovely
lucre than just about anything else.

> I can't afford to work for only ten thousand dollars
> a week.
>
> *Mary Pickford to Adolph Zukor*

> £40 000 a year is a moderate income – such as a
> man might jog on with.
>
> *John George Lambton, First Earl of*
> *Durham*

And that back in 1821!

> The budget for my next film is only 1 500 000
> dollars. A paltry sum.
>
> *Steven Spielberg, about a 'B' film he was*
> *making after* Close Encounters of the
> Third Kind

> It's a terribly hard job to spend a billion dollars
> and get your money's worth.
>
> *George Humphrey*

> Your standard of living varies very little between
> one million and two million.
>
> *Jim Slater*

£477 000 a year is fair for the job.

> *Sir Leslie Smith, chairman of British*
> *Oxygen, of his American chief executive,*
> *Dick Giordano, 1982*

£300 000 would only make you comfortable for two years at the most.

> *Nicholas Coral, 1980*

Football doesn't pay much.

> *Johann Cruyff, Dutch soccer star, on*
> *signing a £290 000 seven-year contract,*
> *1973*

We do everything we can to keep Althorp going and all we get back is a pittance – 6000 visitors a year at £1 a head. Of course, we had a bit of luck with Diana – but all the extra visitors have cracked the library ceiling.

> *Raine Spencer, stepmother of Princess*
> *Diana*

If you live a gilt-edged life, it's difficult to work out just what money means.

A lot of people in the house want to make phone calls, often long distance ones. It mounts up to a pretty substantial sum.

> *J. Paul Getty, on why he was installing a*
> *coin phone in his Sutton Place, Surrey,*
> *mansion*

Ten pounds was like a million dollars. I could spend it on what I liked – cakes and beans.

> *Gilbert O'Sullivan, millionaire pop star.*
> *He told the London High Court his*
> *manager only allowed him pocket money*
> *of £10 a week*

Well, money does bring out the philosopher in people.

My gold came from God.

John D. Rockefeller

Nobody ever feels rich.

Esther Rantzen

It's hard nowadays for a man with five children
and eleven servants to make a living.

Franklin D. Roosevelt

Now my life will be very comfortable as opposed to
comfortable.

*Company director Ted Rumble, August
1983, after £675 720 pools win*

I've got you a million bucks up front, kid. I'm
sorry it's so low, but business is bad these days.

*Mort Janklow, agent, to Shirley Conran,
on selling the follow-up to* Lace

My remuneration is adequate.

*Tom Jones, singer. His last known
earnings, in 1979, were 200 000 dollars a
week*

But you know these showbiz types.

I used to buy clothes in thrift shops. Now I don't
go there because people bother me. Besides, they've
gone up.

Barbra Streisand

Said Jack Dunnett, President of the English Football
League, rejecting a £5 300 000 joint offer by BBC and ITV to
screen soccer for two years:

It was derisory.

Said a Shell executive when the North Sea oil price sagged
three dollars a barrel in February 1983:

We need a petrol price of 178p a gallon before we
start making money again.

The seventies were a bit of a down period. I really had no money!

Mick Jagger

Martina Navratilova, who in 1983 made £60 000 out of a total Wimbledon prize fund of £987 211, talked of a boycott of the 1984 event, saying:

The prize money is pathetic. Players are just pulling in nothing, or next to nothing.

15
WAR AND PEACE

'I've come to the conclusion that there is no way to win the war,' said Richard Nixon on Vietnam. 'But we can't say that, of course. In fact, we have to say the opposite, just to keep some degree of bargaining leverage.' War is created by lies, is run on deceit, and ends with forlorn excuses. Senator Hiram Johnson came up with the most widely quoted maxim: 'The first casualty when war comes is truth.' Sun-tzu in *The Art of War* put it more succinctly: 'All warfare is based on deception.' How right he was.

Few can forget today the forked tongues of Indo-China:

> Our diplomatic reports indicate that the opposing forces no longer really expect a military victory in South Vietnam.
>
> *Lyndon B. Johnson, on the stump, 1966*

> Our staying power is what counts in the long and dangerous months ahead. The Communists expect us to lose heart . . . they believe political disagreements in Washington, and confusion and doubt in the United States, will hand them victory in South Vietnam. They are wrong.
>
> *Lyndon B. Johnson, July 1967*

> Australian troops in Vietnam really have their tails up . . . . Where six months ago there was doubt, there is no doubt now that the Communists have had it.
>
> *Rt. Rev. H.R. Gough, Archbishop of Sydney, back from the front, November 1965*

> The war is not a stalemate. We are winning slowly but steadily.
>
> *Gen. William Westmoreland, July 1967*

The enemy is tactically defeated.
>   *Walt Rostow, L.B.J. aide, April 1968*

Don't just blame the Americans. Through the Vietnam war, Hanoi maintained a policy of blanket lying, including claims that there were no North Vietnamese troops in South Vietnam, they were not getting arms from China and the Soviet Union, and there were no supply lines through, or bases in, Laos or Cambodia.

Then when the dubious Paris 'peace' agreement was signed:

> Our people, raising high the banner of peace and national concord, have decided to apply strictly the clauses of the agreement, in order to maintain peace, independence and democracy and to progress towards the peaceful reunification of their country.
>>   *Le Duc Tho, Hanoi's chief negotiator,*
>>   *January 1973*

> The reunification of Vietnam will take place in stages through peaceful means, on the basis of discussions and agreements between North and South Vietnam, without coercion, or annexation of one party by the other, and without foreign interference. The time limit for reunification will be determined by agreement between North and South Vietnam.
>>   *Le Duc Tho again*

But such is the level of deceit, those in charge sometimes manage to confuse even themselves.

When, in August 1983, the first US peacekeeping troops were killed in Beirut, some members of Congress wanted to bring them home under the War Powers Act. But the White House ruled:

> This is not war. The marines are not in combat.

Yes, they were dying. Yes, they were firing back. But:

> The crucial point is they are in a stationary position.

Ah, like in the trenches.

I don't know what is to be done. This isn't war.
Field Marshal Lord Kitchener, 1914

We are not at war with Egypt. We are in armed conflict.

Anthony Eden, British PM, 1956, during the Suez Crisis

The official verdict on the Korean War (1950–53) was that it was:

A police action.

On the UN side alone, there were 76 000 killed, 250 000 wounded, and 83 000 missing or captured.

We are not in a war situation.
Ministry of Defence spokesman on the Falklands, May 1982

Deception in warfare is often justified. It saves lives. To protect the D-day landings, the Allies mounted the greatest deception in history with phoney armies, inflatable tanks, bogus convoys, dummy parachutists – even an SAS team with record players, loudspeakers, and firecrackers creating a mock 'battle' away from the real action.

During the Falklands 'situation' British Defence chief Sir Frank Cooper not only managed to keep the Argentine fleet in harbour with a false rumour that the nuclear sub, HMS Superb, was in the South Atlantic. He also misled the world at a press briefing the night before British troops went ashore, saying:

> I do not expect a D-day landing.

This was flashed around the world. The Argentines were unprepared. And an unrepentant Sir Frank was left to defend his remark:

> It was not a D-day landing. A D-day landing is actually an *opposed* landing and I know what I'm talking about because I was on one.

Even so, British attempts to fog the enemy over the Falklands were nothing compared with the lies put out by official and unofficial Argentine spokesmen, who claimed between them:

> Eleven Harriers downed
> HMS Hermes sunk (three times)
> HMS Invincible sunk (four times)
> Canberra with 3000 troops aboard sunk (three times)
> British marines drunk and unable to fight
> Crew of HMS Hermes mutinied
> Task Force commander Admiral Sandy Woodward dead – suicide

That sort of thing doesn't confuse the enemy, of course – it just totally misleads the public. Which is why US Secretary of the Navy Col. Frank Knox came under fire after Pearl

Harbour. He admitted one battleship, the Arizona, had been lost, and another, the Oklahoma, had capsized but could be righted. But, he said, the bulk of the Pacific Fleet:

> . . . with its aircraft carriers, heavy cruisers, light cruisers, destroyers and submarines is uninjured and all at sea seeking contact with the enemy.
>
> *16 December 1941*

Note he didn't mention 'battleships' in his list. Catastrophically, another three had been sunk and another three damaged. Was he trying to confuse the Japanese (they knew, of course, how many ships they'd sunk) . . . or the American public?

Information *is* difficult to come by in wartime, while the public thirst for details is insatiable. The result is more confusion, as in this see-saw series of splash headlines from *The Sun* during the Falklands episode:

IT'S WAR!	April 3
PEACE IS IN THE AIR	April 12
FULL AHEAD FOR WAR	April 14
VICTORY	April 26
OUR DARKEST HOUR	May 27
WE'VE WON	June 15

It's been the same through history, of course. In the two years from November 1917 the *New York Times* reported on no fewer than 91 occasions that the Bolsheviks were beaten or about to be beaten. Among the news items:

Petrograd fallen (six times)
Petrograd about to fall (three times)
Petrograd burned to the ground (twice)
Petrograd up in arms against the Bolsheviks (six times)
Population starving to death (seventeen times)

Lenin, too, was the subject of not-too-accurate reports in a variety of journals:

1918	January 17	Four shots fired at Lenin
	February 18	Attempt to kidnap him
	February 20	He'd fled
	March	He'd dismissed Trotsky
	June 29	Moscow captured, Red leaders flee
	August 12	Lenin in flight, 'Red regime totters'
	August 13	In flight again
	October 26	Lenin in peril
	December 9	Red leaders ready to flee to Sweden
	December 16	Lenin about to give up
1919	January 9	Trotsky has Lenin jailed
	January 16	Lenin in Barcelona
	January 20	Definite break between Lenin and Trotsky
	May 28	Red leaders in flight again

For Britain, the worst day ever came at the Battle of the Somme in July 1916. The war correspondents reported it:

Victory, with only slight losses.

Twenty thousand British men were killed and 60 000 wounded. In the newspapers the day was described as:

On balance, a good day for England.

Propaganda is always the name of the game.

Germany has no intention of attacking Belgium or France. Owing to the gigantic armaments of France and the enormous fortifications on the French eastern frontier, such an attack would be pointless from a military point of view.

Adolf Hitler, 1934

The campaign in the East has been decided by the smashing of the Timoshenko Army Group. Further developments will take place as we wish them to happen. Through the last immense blows inflicted by us on the Soviet Union she is finished militarily. The English dream of war on two fronts has definitely come to an end.

Otto Dietrich, Hitler's press chief, October 1941

To some, of course, war is an addiction . . . if you can believe what they say:

War is the most exciting and dramatic thing in life. In fighting to the death you feel terribly relaxed when you manage to come through.

Gen. Moshe Dayan

Aside from being tremendous it was one of the most aesthetically beautiful things I have seen.

Donald Hornig, head of the Manhattan project, on the first atom bomb test

War is good for you.

Tim Page, British war photographer

Some say there are more traumatic things in life . . . if you can take *their* word.

War is a very rough game but I think politics is worse.

Field Marshal Lord Montgomery

Politics are almost as exciting as war, and quite as dangerous. In war, you can only be killed once, but in politics, many times.

Winston Churchill

If I had a son I'd prefer he went to war than to play soccer. There are terrible battles in soccer, worse than war itself.

Santiago Bernabeu, Spanish soccer club president

Though the busiest forked tongues of combat are always those of the losers:

> It is true that we have reached final victory but we have repeatedly warned our readers against believing that fighting is over.
>> Berliner-Lokal-Anzeiger, *October 1942*

ENGLISH DEFEAT.
>> *Splash headline in* Diario Popular,
>> *Argentine newspaper, May 1982*

> This is not a rout. This is a planned withdrawal.
>> *Andrew Peacock, Australian army*
>> *minister, on pull-out from Vietnam*

And the all-time world war classic:

> The war situation has developed, not necessarily to Japan's advantage.
>> *Japanese imperial transcript announcing*
>> *the surrender, 1945*

16
DOUBLESPEAK, KREMLINSPEAK, HAIGSPEAK

'I wouldn't put it as a riot situation – it's a major disturbance situation,' said a Miami police spokesman. 'Just because a programme gets a zero rating doesn't mean a lot of people aren't watching it,' said a spokesman for Channel 4 TV.

Pioneered by the military. Nurtured by increasing government desire to 'fog' the public. Doublespeak has become not only an American, but a world growth industry these past fifteen years.

It's the 1980s way to mislead. The object is to confuse, to bend the truth with a barrage of buzz words. US Commerce Secretary Malcolm Baldrige tried to outlaw the practice. But he was left an incredible legacy by former Secretary of State Alexander Haig.

'Haigese' in fact won for its founder the 1981 Doublespeak award, given by the US national council of teachers of English.

The then-Secretary of State suggested three nuns and a lay worker murdered in El Salvador had angered their killers, by trying to get through a roadblock:

> . . . and this could have been at a very low level of competence and motivation in the context of the issue itself. But the facts on this are not clear enough for anyone to draw a definite conclusion.

Especially if Al Haig is presenting them.

Earlier Doublespeak award winners were the US energy industry, for some hot buzz jargon, including:

> Energetic disassembly

Meaning nuclear explosion. And:

> Rapid oxidation.

Meaning fire.

Another winner was President Carter who called the failed attempt to rescue the Iranian hostages.

An incomplete success.

But it's still the US military that everyone loves to quote.

It became necessary to destroy the town in order to save it.

US army report on the razing of Ben Tre, 1968

We do not hit civilian targets. Correction. We do not target civilian targets.

Pentagon spokesman

We are conducting limited duration protective reaction air strikes.

US army spokesman

In other words, dropping bombs.

Ronald Reagan raised the stakes by calling the deadly intercontinental MX nuclear missile

Peacekeeper.

The White House is to Doublespeak rather what the Louvre is to painting, or Wimbledon is to tennis.

> All agencies with employees having access to classified information will be required to assure that their policies permit us of polygraph examination under carefully designed circumstances. Employees may be required to submit to polygraph tests in the course of investigation of unauthorised disclosures of classified information. This raises the minimum floor of government regulation on polygraphs to require as a minimum an agency has to amend its regulations at least to permit questioning limited to the scope of the unauthorised disclosure.
>
> *Presidential directive, November 1982*

In other words, if there's a leak, you're going to have to take a lie test.

Why use ten short words when a hundred long ones will do? Other US government departments have naturally followed suit.

There is a growing trend towards disregard for the
principle of voluntary tax compliance.

*US General Accounting Office, press
statement*

In other words, there are more income-tax cheats.

Correction: for 'duplicity' read 'duplication'.

*US Transportation Department press
release*

I preferred it the other way round.
  Nevertheless, Alexander Haig, with his triple helping of
Doublespeak training – US military, bureaucracy, and White
House – still leads the field.

Let's push this to a lower decibel level of public
fixation.

He meant let's try to fog the public.

This vortex of cruciality.

He meant row.
  Here's a quick *Forked Tongues* guide to some of the most
outrageous examples of Doublespeak today:

What they say. . .	*What they mean. . .*
emergent nation	backward country
aerial reconnaissance/ reconnaissance in force/ air support	bombing
incontinent ordnance	bombing of schools, hospitals etc. by mistake
warrantless investigation/ uncontested physical search/surreptitious entry	break-in
highly confidential source	bug
plumber	burglar

intelligence gathering/black bag job/covert operation/technical trespass	burglary
negative patient outcome	death
terminal living	dying
hit/executive action	execution
authentic reproduction	fake
pacification	genocide
machine politician	hatchet man
active defence	invasion
account for	kill
categorical inaccuracy	lie
mail cover	mail opening
casualty	murder victim
selective ordnance	napalm
core rearrangement	nuclear accident
gadget	nuclear bomb
collateral damage	nuclear devastation
episode	nuclear near-disaster
event	nuclear disaster
superprompt critical power excursion	nuclear meltdown
plausible denial	official lying
separate development	racialism
negative economic growth	recession
retrograde manoeuvre	retreat
dehired, selected out	sacked
outplacement/decruitment/ constructive termination	sacking
misunderstanding	screw-up
reconnaissance	search and destroy mission
freedom fighter	terrorist
advanced defence condition	war

Doublespeak has, of course, gone international – in a big way. The Israelis called their 1982 flattening of West Beirut:

Peace for Galilee.

While a Pakistani army spokesman defended their 'takeover' in these words:

> I wouldn't describe it as a coup. It's more of an interregnum.
>
> *Pakistan army colonel, 1967*

Then there are the Italians.

> At this moment we are not in crisis. But substantively we are very close to it.
>
> *Italian government press spokesman*

Academics have a case to answer, too.

> Jimmy Carter may have won the 1976 election. But he lost the campaign.
>
> *Edwin Diamond*

And when academics go into politics . . .

> If you buy land on which is a slagheap 120 feet high and it costs £100 000 to remove it, that is not speculation but land reclamation.
>
> *Harold Wilson, defending friends' controversial land deal*

> What we are trying to do is go straight down the road in a four dimensional situation.
>
> *Harold Wilson again*

Then there's Willie Whitelaw.

> We are examining alternative anomalies.

> I don't blame anyone, except, perhaps, all of us.

But let's not be too hard on Americans and British. If you want real Doublespeak, go behind the iron curtain.

> The Soviet Union offered fraternal internationalist assistance to the Czechoslovak people.
>
> *Czech Communist central committee*

We call them tanks.

Then there's Islamic Doublespeak (it's a bit more veiled).

> The Kurds who are being executed do not belong to the Kurdish people.
>
> *Ayatollah Khomeini*

They'll feel a lot better for that.

> You have to treat death like any other part of life.
>
> *Tony Sneva, US racing driver*

> I was banned for life, for a while.
>
> *Jeff Thomson, Australian fast bowler (he ko'ed a soccer referee)*

> The Communist Party of the Soviet Union considers it its internationalist duty to contribute in every way to strengthening the Czechoslovak Communist Party, preserving and consolidating socialism in Czechoslovakia and defending it against the scheming of imperialism.
>
> *Pravda*

In a word: invasion.

There is a lighter side to Doublespeak, of course.

> Cocaine isn't habit forming. I know – I've been taking it for years.
>
> *Tallulah Bankhead*

> It was like the 60s, but it wasn't the 60s. It was 1969.
>
> *Jimmy Savile*

> **REAGAN HAS NEVER BEEN MADDER**
>
> *Headline on article about 'US anger' in* The Observer

> Bachelor, 40, non-driver, would like to accompany same on car tour of Ireland.
>
> *Ad. in* Belfast Newsletter

On Location, the newsletter of the Camera Users' Club, informed members in one issue that:

> Our Girl Friday mans the phones between 9 a.m. and 12 noon on Tuesdays and Thursdays.

Though my favourite official Doublespeak remains this notice affixed to an electricity pylon:

> BEWARE! TO TOUCH THESE WIRES IS INSTANT DEATH. Anyone found doing so will be prosecuted.

17
THAT'S SHOWBIZ

'My flirting days are over,' announced a young, blonde, nineteen-year-old actress called Susan George in September 1970. That was, of course, before well-publicised friendships with John Lloyd, Jimmy Connors, Michael Crawford, Gavin Hodge, Jack Jones, Rod Stewart, Tony Monopoly, Ben Thomas, Prince Charles and Simon MacCorkindale. 'We can never understand all this fuss about him' said Mr Joe Jagger of his son, Michael. 'He really is a very serious boy.'

There's no business like show business when it comes to romanticising, storytelling, putting a false face on things . . . .

> I am very much in love with Leslie Caron and that's something that won't change.
>> *Warren Beatty, 1965. (Bring on Natalie Wood, Joan Collins, Joni Mitchell, Carly Simon, Goldie Hawn, Julie Christie, Diane Keaton, Liv Ullman, Old Uncle Tom Cobbleigh . . .)*

> I know when I married Peter Sellers I said I would be married for ever. And that was my intention and certainly what I wanted. Now I want Lou Adler and me to be together for ever and I think we will.
>> *Britt Ekland*

Well, it did last five months.

> The idea we're together is garbage and nonsense.
>> *Billy Connolly on Pamela Stephenson, May 1981*

> These rumours are all absolute nonsense.
>> *Billy Connolly on Pamela Stephenson, July 1981*

Finally they came clean, and admitted it.

110

In November 1982, Joan Collins said of suggestions she was splitting from her husband, Ron Kass:

> There is not a shred of truth in these rumours.

Said Mr Kass:

> My ankle is broken – but not our marriage.

They separated three months later.

In March 1983, Richard Grant, press agent for *Dallas* star Linda Gray spoke on rumours she was splitting from her spouse, Ed Thrasher:

> They are absolute rubbish.

Mr Grant announced the break-up just two weeks later.

> Superstar Warren Beatty, the bachelor king of Hollywood, has been hooked at last. And yesterday Beatty and the girl who tamed him, Michelle Phillips, flew to the island of Bali for a secret wedding.
>
> *Piers Akerman,* The Sun, *June 1975*

Oh no they didn't.

> I'll never marry again.

Said Reginald Bosanquet after divorce from his wife Felicity in 1975. (He did, to estate agent Joan Adams.)

> I'll never marry again.

Said singing star Cher after her divorce from husband Sonny. (She did, to rock star Greg Allman.)

> I'll marry Paul McCartney this year.
>
> *Jane Asher, 1967*

> If I marry anyone it'll be Jane Asher.
>
> *Paul McCartney, 1967*

> I really love Anouk Aimée and I want to spend all my time with her.
>
> *Ryan O'Neal, 1975*

Why are they always so definite?

> I'll never play another concert after the age of 33.
>
> *Mick Jagger*

> I'll never work for Paramount again.
>
> *Ryan O'Neal after* Love Story. *He was back 12 months later for* Paper Moon

> I wouldn't act again. Not for anything. I don't want to be looked upon as a pretty, brainless idiot any more.
>
> *Victoria Principal, 1976. She later became Pam Ewing in* Dallas

We've already seen how the stars all lie about their age. Here's more on the same subject.

> I can't wait to be 35.
>
> *Glenda Jackson*

> At 36, I think I've had my day.
>
> *Lewis Collins*

Glenda again:

> The successful woman today has to be blonde with big breasts and a maddening giggle.
>
> *Glenda Jackson*

But where does that put Mrs Thatcher?

> They really aren't so big. In such an itty bitty thing like I'm wearing, they just look bigger than they are.
>
> *Dolly Parton*

Ah, these sex symbols. They're so *modest* with it.

Somewhere deep down inside me I feel there's a really good film to be made so I just keep scratching and digging, hoping the next one will be the one.

Burt Reynolds

I just grope along from day to day, feeling my way.

Jacqueline Bisset

I'm the oldest whore in the business.

Robert Mitchum

She's just an ordinary kid.

'Aunt' Lila Wisdom, Paramount chaperone to Brooke Shields

Some days I detest what I see in the mirror.

Raquel Welch

I was never beautiful, I was just pretty. I am ugly now. I do not sunbathe in the nude because I would not inflict this sight on anybody.

Brigitte Bardot, aged 48

I loathe and hate my body. My bottom is too fat, my legs too short, even my back is fat.

Jill Gascoigne

Can you believe what the celebrities tell you?

I formed the Ant group as a declaration against all the crap that had been heaped upon me and young people for what we are. I became a warrior against ignorance.

Adam Ant

He made a bit of money, too.

I'm a real librarian at heart – very shy.

Bette Midler

Apart from his little idiosyncracies, he comes across as a regular sort of chap.

Pauline McLeod, Daily Mirror, *on Boy George*

And if that's one of show business's immortal lines, what about movie director Victor Fleming. Rejecting David O. Selznick's offer of a percentage of the profits rather than a salary on his new film, he is the man who said:

Don't be a damned fool, David. *Gone With the Wind* is going to be one of the biggest White Elephants of all time.

18
U-TURNS

'Nobody talks about a weak Carter any more,' wrote Nicholas Von Hoffman in the *Spectator* on 1 November 1980, when the weekly prematurely awarded a second term to the peanut farmer from Plains.

Lo and behold, in the very next issue, a leading article fumed: 'Mr James "Jimmy" Carter has surely been the most inadequate American president for several generations. . . even the despised Hoover and Nixon. . . none can be ranked as low as this shifty, helpless, ruthless but clumsy man whose main talent was for deceiving the electorate and for deceiving himself. . . .'

Not to mention the *Spectator*.

This is a catalogue of U-turns. Volte-faces. And words not so much eaten as gulped down whole.

While on the subject of Citizen Carter, he announced in November 1977:

> I'm proud of my brother. I have never had any occasion to be embarrassed by Billy.

By January 1979, he was singing a different tune:

> You know, family matters and my brother Billy are fairly sensitive with me. I have no control over Billy.

And in October 1982, he finally admitted:

> The issue of Billy and his work for the Libyans hurt me.

So much for his promise never to tell a lie!

But politics is a world of spectacular second thoughts. As Ian Smith said:

> Mugabe is a Marxist terrorist.

Not to mention:

> An apostle of Satan.

But then, when Mugabe took power, Mr Smith cooed:

> He's sober and responsible. He's a pragmatist.

And even:

> Mr Mugabe's government will probably be the best in Africa.

Politicians have short memories. Ask Alexander Haig.

> I'm in control here.
> > *TV broadcast, March 1981, after Reagan*
> > *assassination attempt*

> There is really only one spokesman for American foreign policy, and it is President Reagan.
> > *Alexander Haig, February 1982*

'I'm in charge' are every Secretary of State's famous last words.

> I've always acted alone. Americans like that enormously.
> > *Henry Kissinger, in famous 'Lone Ranger'*
> > *interview, November 1972*

> How could I ever give such an interview?
> Me, I can't even ride a horse.
> > *Henry Kissinger, December 1972*

Nixon had hit the roof. Henry had once said of him:

> Nixon isn't fit to be President.

And then took the job. Just as George Bush called Reaganomics:

> Voodoo economics.

It didn't stop him making for the White House either.

Both might claim that history proved them right in the end. British politicians, by contrast, almost always finish being proved *wrong* in the end.

> I see no reason why the mass of British industry should find itself short of money this coming year.
>
> *Denis Healey, on coming to office as Chancellor of the Exchequer, 1974*

> There is a collapse of business confidence in Britain.
>
> *Denis Healey, after six months as Chancellor, September 1974*

Or, at least, they change their minds. (My italics below.)

> *Socialist* values and attitudes will only bear fruit in Britain, as in continental Europe, with a sustained period over ten years of *socialist* government.
>
> *David Owen,* Face the Future, *hardback edition*

> *Social Democratic* values and attitudes will only bear fruit in Britain, as in continental Europe, with a sustained period over ten years of government.
>
> *David Owen,* Face the Future, *paperback edition*

> There is no way I could have been anything but a socialist. It would have been a clear revolt against my whole upbringing and family background.
>
> *Shirley Williams, 1980*

Then there are Kinnockisms.

> In reality he is kind, scholarly, innocuous – and as weak as hell.
>
> *Neil Kinnock, on Michael Meacher,* Mail on Sunday, *25 September 1983*

> Of Mr Meacher I said he is kind and
> scholarly – which means that others would think of
> him as innocuous and weak as hell.
>
> *Neil Kinnock,* Daily Mail, *26 September,*
> *1983*

OK, try putting your tongue round both of those and make your own mind up which he actually said!

Talking of double acts, take Sebastian Coe and Steve Ovett, stars of the 1980 Moscow Olympics.

Coe on the 800 metres:
800 metres still has to be my number one target and I'm not displeased that that race comes first.

Ovett on the 800 metres:
I don't like the distance. The race is over too quickly for me.

Ovett on the 1500 metres:
The 1500 is the one I'm really prepared for. It's the one I want. Steve Ovett is a miler. I've got a 50 per cent chance of winning the 800 metres, and a 90 per cent chance of winning the 1500.

Needless to say, it was the other way round. Ovett won the 800 metres and Coe the 1500.

A NEW BEGINNING

> *Ed Muskie (Democrat) campaign slogan,*
> *1972*

A NEW BEGINNING

> *Ronald Reagan (Republican) campaign*
> *slogan, 1980*

In America, old slogans never die. They just find new candidates.

In Britain, the candidates stay the same. It's just the policies which do a quick about-turn.

We believe the British Government has sought membership of the EEC in a manner fully in accord with the principles and objects of the Labour Party. That is why the Labour Party fully supports Britain's application to join the EEC.

> *Resolution passed by the Labour Party Conference, 1967, before de Gaulle's second 'non'*

A profound political mistake made by the Heath Government was to accept the terms of entry to the Common Market and to take us in without the consent of the British people.

> *Labour programme, October 1973*

Ask left Labour star Anthony Wedgwood – sorry, Tony Benn:

I can see really significant long-term opportunities for ordinary people in Britain and in the Six if we could persuade the British public to vote for entry.

> *Speech at Bristol, July 1971*

But as well as his name, he changed his mind!

Britain's continuing membership of the Community would mean the end of Britain as a completely self-governing nation and the end of our democratically-elected parliament as the supreme law-making body in the United Kingdom.

> *Letter to constituents, December 1974*

He's not the only one.

I'm now satisfied that the documents are authentic.

> *Lord Dacre, 23 April 1983*

There is a possibility that the documents were forged.

> *Lord Dacre, 24 April 1983*

I now understand that the link between the plane and the documents is not quite as I thought.

> *Lord Dacre on the 'Hitler Diaries',*
> *25 April 1983*

Oops!

The social contract is central to this Government's policy. To contemplate what would happen under the Opposition's proposals that would break the social contract and add hugely to inflation is to realise the sort of problems the country would face.

> *Joel Barnett, Chief Secretary to the*
> *Treasury, October 1976*

The disastrous social contract may have helped secure our election victory, but it did nothing to prevent – some may argue that it ensured – the 27 per cent growth in earnings that followed.

> *Joel Barnett, February 1982*

It's not always the politicians.

This is the run-up to the big match which, in my view, should be a walkover.

> *Rear Admiral Sandy Woodward, British*
> *Task Force Commander South Atlantic,*
> *April 1982*

Unless people say let's stop, it will be a long and bloody campaign.

> *Rear Admiral Sandy Woodward, May 1982*

I never believed it would be a walkover.

> *Rear Admiral Sandy Woodward, July 1982*

Talking of guns and all that:

Perhaps it is worth mentioning that a new editor of *Shooting Times* has been appointed. This is Philip Brown, who for 17 years previously was secretary of the Royal Society for the Protection of Birds.

> *The Observer*

People will change their minds.

Following our 'Every girl's guide to top glamour boys' in which G_____ was described as a 'tantalising tease' we would like to make it clear that he is happily married and it was not our intention to suggest any impropriety. We apologise for any embarrassment which we may have caused to him or his wife.

Apology in the Sunday People

19
TWENTY-FOUR LIES FOR GATECRASHING THE BIG EVENT

Definitely *not* worth using:

> Nice to see you on the door again, Fred.
> *My name's Jack, an' always 'as bin.*
> You'll never believe this. . . .
> *No, sir, I won't.*
> Don't you know who I am?
> *Who the bloody 'ell are you, sir?*
> I left my ticket at the station by mistake – can I get in on a BR cheap day return?

However, some of these *have* been known to work:

1 I'm with Adnan Khashoggi's party.
2 Princess Margaret's got the invitations – she's following on behind.
3 Does the word 'Mafiosi' mean anything to you?
4 I'm the Marquess of Bute.
5 I'm the Marquis de Sade.
6 Shiver me timbers! I must have left the tickets in me Rear-Admiral's uniform.
7 I left the tickets at Annabel's. You couldn't be a dear old thing and go and get them for me, could you?
8 I left the tickets at Brown's, or if I'd had any tickets, I would have left them at Brown's.
9 They must have sent the tickets to the Palace by mistake.
10 They must have sent the tickets to the Palais by mistake.
11 The invitation was so grand, I decided to have it framed.
12 I've been thrown out of better places than this.
13 I've been let into better places than this.

14 I'm undercover for the SAS, but don't tell the waiters.

15 I'm undercover for Egon Ronay, and make sure you tell the waiters.

16 But Jimmy Connors said he'd leave the tickets here for me.

17 Has my friend Mr Kray arrived yet?

18 I'm with Boy George, but he's still doing his face.

19 I'm with Mari Wilson, but she's still doing her hair.

20 I'm with Barbra Streisand, but she's still powdering her nose.

21 Any trouble and I'll send for my lawyer – Marvin Mitchelson.

22 I'm Morgan Fairchild in drag.

23 Surely guests of honour don't have to show invitations?

24 I'm only here for the Gay Gordons.

20
NUMBER 1 LIES

'I have been put here by the Gods in the sky. Bullets bounce off me, I am invincible,' said the patron saint of the humble, Idi Amin. But there's another side to the coin. 'This rarely happens to an ordinary fellow like me,' said Aristotle Onassis on being taken to lunch by Churchill and Macmillan. 'Me, I'm just Mr Average,' says Barry Manilow.

So many lies are told about 'Number 1' – the ego – they could fill a book in themselves. As you see, they fall into two categories. First the boasting and bragging of big mouths, like Amin. And second (and these are the lies no one minds) the self-effacement of genuinely modest men and women.

No need to say to which category these belong:

> I know that during my long life I have always been right about what I said.
> *Ayatollah Khomeini*

> I often quote myself. It adds spice to the conversation.
> *George Bernard Shaw*

> I have not addressed such a distinguished audience since dining alone in the hall of mirrors.
> *Henry Kissinger, at first historic meeting of Washington ambassadors of Egypt and Israel*

> I only work according to God's instructions. It is the voice of God, not just me speaking.
> *Idi Amin*

> My face is the most beautiful face in the world.
> *Idi Amin again*

How pleasant it is to listen to those whose pronouncements lie in the other direction:

> What I have done personally is much exaggerated.
> *Albert Einstein*

I just put my feet in the air and wiggle them around.

Fred Astaire

It's tough at the top.

A psychologist in Cambridge, Mass., has as a patient a person named Superman: he thinks he's Henry Kissinger.

Washington joke

I don't care how many prima donnas there are as long as I'm the prima donna absoluta.

Gough Whitlam

I'm a little smarter than people give me credit for.

Billy Carter

Wanna bet?

I have made six hundred speeches for Jimmy. I couldn't have made that many without being good.

'Miz' Lillian Carter

I am one of the best coaches and teachers of the game in the world. I was too good for English football. That's why they kicked me out.

Malcolm Allison

I don't try to be Joe Blow the superstud. It just happens.

Jeff Thomson

I am the world's greatest politician. America has asked me to help them in Vietnam. I have offered my help to Britain to solve the Ulster problem.

Idi Amin

(His solution: shoot everyone, then they wouldn't fight quite as much.)

No, I think we're all on the side of the little man.

I think and think, for months, for years. Ninety-nine times the conclusion is false. The hundredth time I am right.

Albert Einstein

Or little woman.

I am just an average woman who has worked hard all her life.

Jacqueline Bisset

Come, come.

I may not be a great actress but I've become the greatest at screen orgasms. Ten seconds of heavy breathing, roll your head from side to side, simulate a slight asthma attack and die a little.

Candice Bergen

Women are definitely worst for hiding their light!

I've got chipmunk cheeks stuffed with nuts.

Jane Fonda

My neck's too long, my hands too big and my voice too small.

Vivien Leigh

I'm attractive *maybe*. My eyes are all make-up. My mouth is too full, my nose is terrible, and my hair is awful.

Jacqueline Bisset

I am not the world's most beautiful woman. I am not! I am an old bag.

Elizabeth Taylor

But it's not just those in Hollywood who play down their roles. Asked how he became a war hero, John F. Kennedy replied:

It was involuntary. They sunk my boat.

Modesty is so infectious.

I am not at all powerful.

Indira Gandhi

I am just a grocer in Britain and America and that's what I intend to remain.

Sir James Goldsmith, millionaire financier

Superman? Are you kidding? I've had allergies and asthma all my life. I'm just an actor.

Christopher Reeve

If only people knew as much about painting as I do, they would never buy my pictures.

Sir Edward Landseer

This 'King' business is all bullshit. I was in the right place at the right time and I had a lot of guys helping me – that's all.

Clark Gable

Others claim to have aid from more divine quarters.

God is on my side and even the most powerful witchcraft cannot hurt me.

Idi Amin

Who says I am not under the special protection of God?

Adolf Hitler after failed attempt on his life, 1944

Hitler was a strong leader like me. But his line was different.

Idi Amin

These days, just who *can* you believe?

Everyone seems obsessed about winning gold medals. I just can't understand it.

Steve Ovett

I am Mr Average.

Lord Grade

I'm just an ordinary bloke.

Robert Muldoon

We're just a bunch of crummy musicians.

George Harrison on the Beatles

Oh *yeah*?

Finally, which direction is this gentleman lying in? Make up your own mind.

I got a momma who joined the Peace Corps when she was 68. I got one sister who's a Holy Roller preacher. Another wears a helmet and rides a motor cycle. And my brother thinks he's going to be President. So that makes me the only sane one in the family.

Billy Carter

Like we said, you wanna bet?

21
LIES, DAMNED LIES. . . .

'Oh, don't tell me of facts,' said Sydney Smith. 'I never believe in facts: you know Canning said nothing was so fallacious as facts, except figures.'

Earl Asquith waxed similar on the three sets of statistics kept by the British war office: 'One to mislead the public, another to mislead the Cabinet, and another to mislead itself.'

Figures have always been so easy to 'bend'.

> 100% talking! 100% singing! 100% dancing!
> *First talkies slogan, 1927*

Something just doesn't add up.

> I am 101% fit.
> *Margaret Thatcher after eye operation,*
> *1983*

> I help make an average family. . . . Jimmy is 100 per cent and I am 0 per cent. So it comes to 50 per cent because of me.
> *Billy Carter*

But what about 'Miz' Lillian?

> Four per cent of nothing is nothing.
> WE WANT TWELVE PER CENT!
> *Banner during health workers' dispute,*
> *1982*

Here's a quick *Forked Tongues* guide to some of the more cunning ways politicians and the civil service confuse us with statistics:

1 The 'At this Moment in Time' Trick

In September 1974, the then Chancellor of the Exchequer, Denis Healey, went on the record as saying:

Inflation is currently running at 8.4 per cent.

And he produced figures to prove it – very handy with an election coming up. And very skilful when the true inflation rate was actually 15.6 per cent.

What Mr Healey did was to take a three-month reading of the retail price index distorted by:

(1)   fresh food prices down for the summer;
(2)   new government subsidies; and
(3)   the lowering of the VAT rate. . . by Mr Healey himself!

Liberal leader Jeremy Thorpe said the Chancellor had applied 'plastic surgery' to the figures. But Healey said Tory claims of an inflation rate of 15-20 per cent were 'a lie'. He later had to eat his words. . . but not until after a Labour Government had been returned to power.

2   The '2 + 2 = 1.5' Trick

On 3 June 1983, six days before the General Election, the Conservative Government released figures for unemployment in Britain of 3 049 351 – down 120 528 on the previous month. Said Chancellor Sir Geoffrey Howe:

The figures represent an improvement.

In fact the dole queues had *increased* by 23 000 in May. As well as a seasonal change not taken into account, what the Government did was to take a whole category of people. . . the over 60s. . . off the unemployment register, ruling they no longer had to 'sign on' to qualify for national insurance credits.

It was one of a series of 'adjustments' to the figures. The previous November, 200 000 unemployed not qualifying for benefit were removed from the register, as were 350 000 in government training schemes. The *Daily Mirror* called it 'The Big Lie' and charged that the Government had 'decided on a series of statistical fiddles' to improve the jobless total. But it worked. The next week the Tory Government was re-elected with a vastly increased majority.

3   The 'Let's Hide This Somewhere and Hope No one Notices' Trick

In April 1983, Pentagon economic boss David Chu promised the Senate Armed Services Committee. . .

A pleasant surprise

. . . with a report on cost-cutting in the services.

American journalists were nonplussed when they were told a massive 11.3 billion dollars had been saved on the US Trident programme. The reason, said the Pentagon hesitantly, was that there would now be eight, not 15, Trident submarines.

Does that mean, asked the astonished journalists, that the West's most important nuclear deterrent force had been slashed virtually in two?

Oh no, said deputy assistant secretary of defense Joseph Kammerer:

The seven remaining submarines have been renamed Trident II and designated as a new programme.

Fine, said the newsmen. *But what's the difference between a Trident I and a Trident II submarine?* Oh, um, well, said Rear-Admiral Frank Kelso. 'Trident II fires a more advanced missile.'

But the submarines are the same? Er, um, yes. 'It's the same submarine.'

The expected cost of building 15 Tridents, far from decreasing sharply, had risen 2.7 billion dollars to 31.1 billion dollars – an increase of 9.5 per cent in just three months.

And yes, someone *had* noticed.

4   Fiddling with the basics (A Government 'Own Goal')

In August 1979, the Tory Government announced a new statistic to replace the monthly retail price index as a measure of inflation. Designated the 'TPI' (Tax and Price Index) it quickly became known as the 'Thatcher Price Index', and the object of some scorn. In governmentspeak, of course, the TPI was

An important new weapon in the Government's strategy for keeping pay increases to levels the country can afford. . . .

Basically, the Conservatives had raised VAT and were pledged to successively lowering income tax. So they juggled about and came up with the TPI which, they thought, would take these changes into account and show a suitably low inflation figure.

The TUC called it 'a fiddle'. Said their assistant general secretary, David Lea: 'People will smell a rat. It is preposterous to fiddle around with price indexes. We hope the Government's decision will not bring all indexes into disrepute.'

What happened, though, was a classic case of a Government stewing in its own statistical soup. Sure enough, in July 1979, the TPI was showing inflation at 13.2 per cent, while the retail price index put the figure at 15.6 per cent. But by June 1981, the TPI was showing an annual inflation rate of 14.9 per cent. . . the retail price index, only 11.3 per cent.

Surprise, surprise, the Government started quoting the 'unrealistic' retail price index once again. The 'Thatcher Price Index' was quietly dropped.

5   Change the computer!

David Stockman was the whizzkid of the new Ronald Reagan administration. At the age of 35, he was catapulted to Director of the Office of Management and the Budget (OMB), controlling much of the US economy. His creed was 'supply side economics', the controversial theory of reducing inflation and boosting growth through tax cuts and a tight money policy. His problem was, as John Anderson said: How can you raise defence spending, cut income tax, *and* balance your budget all at the same time?

Stockman forecast:

A bull market after April 1981 of historic proportions.

But reality began to overtake theory. He had predicted a balanced budget by 1984. Yet no President had managed that feat in the previous 12 years. Sure enough the computer at OMB started to churn out forecast after forecast of huge inflationary deficits.

Our hero thought hard. How could he eliminate these deficits? He had a brainwave. *He changed the computer*.

It's based on valid economic analysis. But it's the inverse of the last four years.

Sure enough, by May 1981, Stockman's new baby was predicting rosy times ahead. He said:

I think we're on the verge of response in the financial markets.

Later there was an urgent reappraisal. . . not least after Stockman disgraced himself with a wildly indiscreet interview to *Atlantic Monthly*, in which he said a recent tax amendment had been nothing but 'a Trojan horse to bring down the top rate'.

Had he been completely wrong? Well, not *quite*.

Supply side was the wrong atmospherics. Not wrong theory or wrong economics, but wrong atmospherics.

And plaintively he added what might be every economist's homily – and the public's verdict too:

> None of us really understands what's going on with all these numbers.

Damned statistics!

22
CALLING THE KETTLE BLACK

'The British and the Americans,' declared Hitler's propaganda chief Dr Joseph Goebbels in 1945, 'are spreading horror stories about the situation in the West.' That for a man so renowned for telling the truth, the whole truth, and nothing but the truth!

'The Margaret Thatcher Conservative Government resorts to repressions against citizens, depriving them of their freedom,' said the Soviet news agency, Tass. 'I gave John Kennedy a sound lecture on morals,' said Judith Exner, the girlfriend who alternated with a Mafia boss.

This is a chapter of pots calling kettles black. Of those who lie about their own faults . . . by seeing them in others. Of those who try to convince us everyone else is wrong . . . and they alone are right.

> The trouble with De Gaulle is he's got the biggest ego in the world.
> *Lyndon B. Johnson*

> An unscrupulous character.
> *Col. Gaddafi on Ronald Reagan*

> Your country is displaying dangerous militaristic tendencies.
> *Andrei Gromyko to Misuo Takashima, Japanese ambassador*

> The Shah has destroyed everything in our country.
> *Ayatollah Khomeini*

Guerrillas led by Joshua Nkomo once shot down an Air Rhodesia Viscount, killing 59, most of them holidaymakers. Said the 'Father of Zimbabwe':

> When civilian aircraft are used for military purposes, then we bring them down.

In 1983, after his Zapu guerrillas were on the receiving end from Robert Mugabe's men, Nkomo had changed his tune:

> We must pull together . . . if there is conflict, you don't settle it by killing each other.

Said James Callaghan in 1976:

> We have lived too long on borrowed time, borrowed money, and even borrowed ideas . . . for too long this country has trodden the primrose path and borrowed money from abroad – it still goes on – instead of grappling with the fundamental problems of British industry.

What he didn't say was that, as Chancellor from 1964 to 1967, he was one of the chief people to blame for it. Perhaps he should have kept his mouth shut.

> I'm incredibly discreet. I only talk about people who've blabbed to the press all their lives.
> *Gossip column luminary Dai Llewellyn*

> What is straight business anyhow? To be honest, it's just a bloody racket.
> *Ronnie Kray*

Remember former Labour Minister John Stonehouse? He took a dead man's identity, feigned suicide, became an international fugitive. Then, finally appearing at the Old Bailey on 21 charges of conspiracy, fraud, theft and forgery, involving £170 000, he proclaimed:

> I became very disillusioned with politics. The promises made in 1964 were not fulfilled and the Government was playing games with the electorate by saying one thing one time and doing another very soon afterwards.

Not like Mr Stonehouse, of course.

Though Edward Heath did once say about politicians:

They're all incompetent.

Except Edward Heath.

The Conservative Government is an organised hypocrisy.

Benjamin Disraeli

Government by second-rate men will be second-rate government.

Ronald Reagan

I don't like strident women.

Margaret Thatcher

No one should try . . . to dictate to other peoples how they should manage their internal affairs. It is only the people of each given state, and no one else, that have the sovereign right to decide their own internal affairs and to establish their own internal laws.

Leonid Brezhnev, July 1975

Poland, Hungary, Czechoslovakia, Afghanistan, Angola . . . the capitalists are the men of real oppression, of course.

The foreign policy of the Reagan Administration is a policy of force, pressure, and blackmail.

Pravda

Traditional parliamentary democracies are among the most tyrannical dictatorships the world has ever known.

Col. Gaddafi, The Green Book

The western Zionist-imperialist news media are committing the most significant oppression and cruelty ever committed against mankind.

Hojatoleslam Moadikhah, Iranian information minister, April 1982

And that's only on the sports pages.

> The aggressive forces of imperialism are raising
> their military preparedness to unprecedented levels.
>> *Leonid Brezhnev, 1982, as the SS-20s went in*

> The English imperialists have no right to speak of
> the rights of man. The world knows their barbarous
> and abject nature.
>> *Pol Pot Government note to UN, 1978*

> He is a destructive person, the terrorist.
>> *Col. Gaddafi on President Reagan*

> Now that Iran has crossed our border, her
> aggressiveness has been proved.
>> *President Saddam Hussain of Iraq (who
>> had crossed Iran's border and attacked two
>> years before)*

> Lies, misrepresentation and concealment of truth
> have become the hallmarks of successive Republican
> and Democratic administrations.
>> *Tass, 1983*

Finally, trigger-happy triple killer Barry Prudham. In 1982 he became Britain's most dangerous gunman before dying in a shootout with police. Afterwards he was remembered by a relative as saying:

> I went on holiday to Central America. But I didn't
> like El Salvador. People were getting shot all
> around us.

23
CAUGHT IN THE ACT

'I have always loved truth so passionately,' wrote that great roué Casanova, 'that I have often resorted to lying as a way of introducing it into minds which were ignorant of its charms.' Chico Marx, when caught by his wife cuddling up to a chorus girl, came up with the celebrated riposte: 'I wasn't kissing her – I was whispering in her mouth.'

This is the greatest test of mettle and imagination. Caught (metaphorically, of course) with one's pants down. Nabbed red handed. Caught in the act.

Pierre Trudeau, accused of uttering an obscenity in Parliament, offered:

> What I said was 'fuddle-duddle'.

A spokesman for Michael Foot, when he appeared untidily dressed at the Cenotaph, claimed:

> He was perfectly properly dressed. He was wearing a dark suit under his [duffel] coat.

John Stonehouse, when caught living under a false name in Australia, said he should be let go, as

> A psychiatrist's report has said that by returning to Britain, I would do myself irreparable psychiatric damage.

Or to put it another way, be thrown in jail.

Being 'copped' by the police for a driving offence is the lie-test most people go through at least once in their lives. Can you beat the Melbourne motorist who, stopped for speeding, claimed:

> I got a sudden attack of cramp and couldn't lift my leg off the accelerator.

Or the Georgia man who told the police patrol:

I was rushing to the service station so I would get there before the brakes finally gave up.

Pop singer Ozzy Osbourne, who, during one particularly memorable performance, bit off the head of a live bat on stage, explained:

You have to do things in this world to make people sit up. It sounds a bit biblical, but I think I'm on a mission.

When fashion designer Zandra Rhodes was questioned about growing cannabis plants in her flat, her solicitor's explanation was:

Her main interest was in the unusual quality of the plants and the way they blended in with the many other plants she had at her flat. Her judgment was impaired by her interest in gardening.

At Houston, Texas, 82-year-old grandmother Laura Clark, accused of growing six 'pot' plants in her back garden, said:

I thought I was growing herbs for my arthritis.

You know these pensioners.

> We had a wonderful thing going before the raid
> stopped it all. Just to see an old boy coming down
> the stairs with a smile on his face, even if he was a
> bit puffed out, it used to give me a glow, it really did.
> *Mrs Cynthia Payne, luncheon voucher sex queen*

But being caught *in flagrante delicto* is the ultimate test of
the powers of invention. School caretaker Terry Wise, 36, told
an industrial tribunal he had not been making love to a
26-year-old lady teacher on a classroom bench.

> We were just caught in an awkward situation.

Rotterdam fisherman Henryk Lietermann came home in the
small hours and told his wife:

> I found a mermaid in my net and had to take her
> back out to sea to the deep fishing grounds.

She hit him with a heavy oar.
A divorce judge heard how an actress arrived home late one
night and her husband barred entry to the bedroom. There
was a girl with him. He told his wife:

> She was only helping hang some curtains.

Said Mr Justice Faulks:

> That may have been right. But it seems an odd time
> of day for that sort of thing.

Another judge heard how a London window cleaner, caught
with a girl in the bedroom with the lights off, said:

> We were playing snooker. The noises you heard
> were expressions of delight or surprise when playing
> a difficult shot.

142

Asked why the woman in question was naked from the waist down, he said:

She was doing some sewing and altering her slacks.

Courtrooms all over the world echo to the pleas of those caught in the act. Said a Londoner accused of stealing a sack of coal:

All I can suggest is that someone put it on my back when I wasn't looking.

Asked why he had staged a 500 dollar hold-up, an Ontario man replied:

So I could qualify for rehabilitation aid later.

Mr Albert Ball, also of Ontario, was charged with stealing nine pints of frozen bull semen. He told the court:

I am not what you call kinky. Some of the lads dared me to do it.

A man who raped a 24-year-old bride on a remote hill footpath claimed:

> It was half a bottle of cough mixture I had earlier. I was only trying to cure a sore throat.

A Manchester gravedigger accused of striking a man with a hammer explained:

> I always wished that if I killed someone, I would do it before the age of 35.

Charles Everett, 20, of Washington, DC, told police he held up liquor stores in the daytime because:

> I'm afraid to be out on the street at night with all that money.

Alfred Madsen, 21, who confessed in a New York court to stealing 3 000 000 dollars worth of gems from a Manhattan jewellers, said:

> I got impatient waiting for my girlfriend to finish in the bath.

Thomas Babble explained to police why he had 3000 boxes of Black Magic chocolates and 753 bottles of gin stored in his warehouse:

> The baby was on the way so we stocked up.

Finally, a 63-year-old man was jailed for three days at Belo Horizonte, Brazil, for biting the thigh of a girl who sat next to him on the bus. He said:

> The Pope was right. Mini-skirts *are* dangerous.

24
GETTING RID

TWELVE LIES FOR GETTING LATE-STAYING GUESTS TO GO HOME

1 Of course we don't want you to go – we always start twitching and coughing around this time.

2 I can't think why it is – we don't usually yawn all the time like this.

3 Isn't it strange how we ran out of drink, ice-cubes, coffee, and wafer mints all at exactly the same time.

4 I do like the McDuffs. They always do the washing up.

5 They're very keen on breaking and entering around here – I'd check your car is all right if I were you.

6 They're very hot on night-time parking around here – I'd check your car hasn't been towed away if I were you.

7 There's just one problem: all the doors are on time locks and you just could get trapped in the bathroom.

8 It's time for the crocodile's 2 a.m. feed. Could you give me a hand?

9 Or would you rather amuse Johnny's pet tarantula while we go out and walk the dog?

10 Have you got any money on you? Brian's just shown me a new version of poker that Ronnie Biggs taught him.

11 Watch out for the soldier ants. They start coming up through the floorboards and looking for a meal around now.

12 I think that's the vampire bats coming in through the kitchen window.

NB *Whatever you do, don't try:*

> If you don't make a move soon, you're going to have to stay the night. (They'll want to stay the night.)
> I've got an early start, 5 a.m. (They'll say, why bother going to bed at all, then?)

And most of all, don't say:

> This is when we start wife swapping. (They're probably secret swingers.)

TWELVE LIES TO END A PHONE CONVERSATION

1 I'll have to go, I'm expecting a call from Hollywood.
2 Got to go, or the potatoes will boil dry.
3 I'll have to go, I'm expecting a dirty phone call.
4 The dog's about to eat her dinner.
5 The dog's about to eat the postman.
6 This is a bad line. (*Make noises, 'Phut phut'.)* See, (*phut phut*) . . . the phone's being tapped.
7 You won't believe just how much I'm earning now . . . .
8 My mother's cooking lunch, and I can't trust her in the kitchen with all those knives and all that garlic.
9 It's started to rain outside. I'd better hang up in case we get electrocuted.

And if you're feeling *really* adventurous, try these:

1 No, I told you I couldn't hear you.
2 I can hear my spongecake burning.

And, the all-time classic (actually used by the author's mother-in-law, to devastating effect):

> I shall have to go now. I can hear the phone ringing!

25
I NEVER SAID THAT,
AND EVEN IF I DID . . . .

According to Margaret Thatcher, 'You don't tell deliberate lies, but sometimes you have to be evasive.' It's no surprise that this has become the eleventh commandment of officialdom. And the first law of government.

This chapter salutes the omnipresent stonewall of bureaucracy. And its favourite and most silken-tongued way to lie: the official denial.

The Manual of Public Relations by Bowman and Ellis sums it up: 'In a democracy, the press has the right to ask questions. However, it does not necessarily have the right to an answer.'

Here is Jones's cynical media-man's guide to denials. Verbal decoys. And government gobbledegook.

Beginning with this classic from Alexander Haig, when asked if it was true he'd called British Foreign Secretary Lord Carrington 'a duplicitous bastard':

Official statement	*Meaning*
I have three things to say. First, *it couldn't have been me,* speaking that clearly.	It was me, speaking not quite that clearly.
Second, *I don't recall* ever having had such exciting staff meetings.	I don't recall because I'm trying hard to forget.
And third, I hope this puts to rest the myth that there is no imagination at the State department.	Of course I called him a 'duplicitous bastard'.

Casting the net more widely:

No comment.	It's true.
The previous statement is inoperative. (*Nixon White House*)	The President lied.

The President mis-spoke on that point. (*Reagan White House*)	The President goofed.
I will not meet King Hussein in Damascus, I have no plans to meet King Hussein in Damascus, I have no intention of meeting King Hussein in Damascus. (*Henry Kissinger*)	I'll meet him in Amman.
I have no plans for sending American troops to El Salvador. (*Ronald Reagan*)	Casper Weinberger has the plans right now.
The President can't do it, he has a busy schedule.	He wants a nap.
The Government did not misjudge the situation. (*Humphrey Atkins, Lord Privy Seal, on the Falklands*)	We didn't even realise there was a situation to misjudge.
The newspapers this morning have created a false impression.	They didn't swallow our PR handout.
I am unaware/I have no knowledge about this.	Because I've just taken a crash course in amnesia.
It seems very unlikely.	But it's true.
There is no immediate danger.	It's just that the whole town may explode.
The public have nothing to fear.	Just the 60 000 or so people in the danger zone.
This is pure speculation/in the realm of speculation/you speculate all you like. (*Buckingham Palace*)	How on earth did you find out?

I did not give James Reston of the *New York Times* an interview. (*Henry Kissinger*)	I talked to him on the telephone.
Among the prisoners, there are no casualties. (*British Defence Ministry spokesman*)	That's not counting those we didn't take prisoner who are dead.
I am not interested in the post.	Unless I get it.
I have not applied for this post.	But I still hope to get it.
We have no further information at present.	Our PR boys are frantically trying to come up with some lies.
I think that answers all your questions.	Let's get out of this press conference before we have to start telling the truth.
This is my final word on the subject.	Unless you schmucks get another question in.
There was no disagreement. Discussions were perfectly amicable. (*British Foreign Office on EEC talks*)	They were at each others' throats. All hell broke loose.
No differences exist. Whatever rifts there are are bound to go. (*Robert Mugabe*)	Especially when we throw them out of the government.
Poland's internal affairs do not concern us. (*Brezhnev, Andropov*)	Unless Jaruzelski fails. Then we send the tanks in.
I am not a dictator. (*Mrs Gandhi, General Zia, Idi Amin, Papa Doc*)	I just insist everyone does as I say.
We can't conceive of any way it's going to happen right now.	It's likely to happen tomorrow.

It's a zero possibility event.   It's definitely going to
                                 happen tomorrow.

Not all denials are Queensbury rules, of course.

> Q. Kid, are you the strangler?
> A. Cut it out.
>> *Malden detective to Albert De Salvo, the*
>> *Boston Strangler*

> This talk about radio-activity is just so much
> nonsense.
>> *Maj.-Gen. Leslie R. Groves, head of the*
>> *Manhattan project, after reports people*
>> *were still dying at Hiroshima, 1945*

On Wednesday 17 October 1962, when a massive airlift of
military aircraft began to MacDill Air Force Base, Florida, a
curious reporter asked: 'Is this anything to do with Cuba?'
Said a USAF press officer:

> Absolutely not.

The following Sunday when 16 newsmen flew into
Roosevelt Roads, Puerto Rico, to watch the mammoth naval
exercise PHIBRIGLEX 62, they expected to see a large fleet
assembled and thousands of US marines. But there wasn't a
ship or a fighting man in sight.
Said a navy spokesman:

> There has been a hurricane. The fleet has been
> scattered all over. We're hoping to get it back again
> Monday morning.

Well, those were the Kennedy years.

> I've never heard of Judith Campbell Exner.
>> *JFK aide Kenny O'Donnell*

> I'm sorry, I don't recall the name.
>> *Evelyn Lincoln*

The only Campbell I know is Campbell's soup.

> *Dave Powers*

Powers later admitted he *did* know her, but was afraid if he admitted it he might lose his job at the Kennedy Memorial Library.

When a massive meltdown shut the Three Mile Island nuclear plant in March 1979, spokesmen came up with an amazing chain reaction of their own – of denials. They included:

We are not at China syndrome level.

And:

It is a normal aberration.

Finally as it became clear much of Pennsylvania was nearly blown sky high, the electric company spokesman Don Curry said:

We now concede that it's not just a little thing.

But, you might say, that's America.

I have no knowledge of any circumstances that could lead to President Nixon's resignation because of Watergate.

> *Spiro T. Agnew*

Don't get the idea that I'm one of those goddam radicals. Don't get the idea that I'm knocking the American system.

> *Al Capone*

I am unaware that I have ever driven faster than 70.

> *Lyndon B. Johnson, inveterate speedster*

He never looked at the speedo.

It does happen in Britain too.

We were in touch with the Governor half an hour ago and he said that no landing had taken place at that time.

> *Humphrey Atkins, Lord Privy Seal, to the House of Commons, six hours after the Argentine invasion*

And around the world.

Lech Walesa is not under arrest. He is staying at a Government guest house.

> *Polish martial law spokesman*

I don't want to be Prime Minister again.

> *Indira Gandhi, 1979*

I don't want always gets.

I have no intention of seeing General Westmoreland leave his command.

> *Lyndon B. Johnson, February 1968*

He did fire Westmoreland – then said he'd made the decision back in January!

Even more of a giveaway are the incomplete (or partial) denials we hear:

> The charges [against Spiro Agnew] are stale and inaccurate in one major respect.
>
> *Richard Nixon, October 1968*

But in every other respect they're true?

> Archie hasn't retired. He just isn't fighting any more.
>
> *Joan Moore, wife and business manager of boxing champ Archie*

> BOB WOODWARD: Have you ever organised wiretaps yourself?
>
> HENRY KISSINGER: Almost never.

Finally, to five-star, all-purpose denials guaranteed to disarm any press tormentor.

> I will not say where I have been, what I've been doing, or where I'm going.
>
> *Spiro T. Agnew*

Though perhaps the best came from solicitor Duncan Mutch of Barnsley, Yorks. Asked about a newspaper report that his client, cricket star Geoff Boycott, had snubbed an Indian minister, cursed the England tour manager, and behaved oddly when presented with a rose, Mutch replied:

> I am sorry, this is a disgusting conversation. If I was commenting on that I would just tell them to burn the ruddy thing . . . I have never had a telephone call like this in the whole of my life. If a man writes stuff like that he wants his head looking at . . .

Said the perplexed newspaperman who put the question:

I am not sure whether to count that as a denial or a refusal to comment.

26
MORE LIES

Poet Laureate Sir John Betjeman always loved Harrow School – so much so, he used to say he went there. (He actually went to Marlborough.) Confronted with his deceit, Betjeman said: 'It is true I went to Harrow in all but fact.'

When Jimmy Carter became US President, he boldly pledged he would never tell a lie. His momma, Miz Lillian, soon torpedoed that one. 'Oh, I'm sure he's had to tell a few white ones along the line, because I told a dozen last night. I'm sure you can find a few flaws. Everyone makes mistakes.'

Like the editor of *The Sun* in October 1982:

> WORLD EXCLUSIVE: PRIDE AND THE
> HEARTBREAK OF TWO VC WIDOWS
> VC Widow Marica McKay fought back her tears
> last night and said: 'I'm so proud of him. His name
> will remain a legend in the history books for ever.'

They made it up.

And talking of making things up:

> The charges against Communism made from a
> religious, a philosophical, and, generally, from an
> ideological standpoint are not deserving of serious
> examination.
> *Karl Marx,* The Communist Manifesto

Did you say Karl or Groucho?

> Leonid Brezhnev will always be remembered by
> mankind as a consistent, ardent, and indefatigable
> fighter for peace and security of nations, for
> removing the danger of world thermonuclear war
> overhanging mankind.
> *Yuri Andropov*

> *STRONGER PLO EMERGES FROM BEIRUT*
> *PLO London newsletter, after ignominious
> evacuation from Lebanon, 1982*

You will be home before the leaves have fallen from the trees.

> *Kaiser Wilhelm to German troops, August 1914*

It is a pity that in the process of their having to leave the country some people have been unfortunate enough to suffer all sorts of inconveniences and some have died. But Nigeria cannot accept responsibility for this.

> *Oga Okwoche, Nigerian ambassador to Paris, on the expulsion of two million Ghanaians, February 1983*

In the USSR and other socialist countries, as distinct from the imperialist states, there are no classes or groups that have any interest in the arms race, or in military preparations.

> *Leonid Brezhnev, December 1977*

I have no interest in making films.

> *Marlon Brando*

I know nothing of high affairs.

> *Christine Keeler*

There is nothing I want so much as an opportunity to retire.

> *Dwight D. Eisenhower, November 1945*

No alert has been ordered nor have any emergency military measures been set in motion against Communist-ruled Cuba. Further, the Pentagon has no information regarding the presence of offensive weapons in Cuba.

> *Pentagon spokesman, October 1962*

We both of us came to the Soviet Union to work for the aim of better understanding between the Soviet Union and the West.

> *Guy Burgess and Donald Maclean, joint statement, 1956*

They won't attack you through the 17th parallel.
You've got plenty of strength to hold them there.
There is nothing to worry about. If they attack, we
will react.

> *Henry Kissinger to Tran Van Lam, South*
> *Vietnamese Foreign Minister, Paris,*
> *January 1973*

In view of the persecution I have received from the
English authorities and the British press, I have
decided to resign from the House of Commons in
due course and renounce my United Kingdom
citizenship.

> *John Stonehouse, letter to Olof Palme,*
> *March 1975*

I can see no reason why this war must go on.

> *Adolf Hitler, after the fall of France*

Our opponents would like to find forces of some
sort opposed to socialism inside our countries. Since
there are no such forces, because in socialist society
there are no oppressed or exploited classes or
oppressed or exploited nationalities, some sort of
substitute has been invented and an ostensible
'internal opposition' in socialist countries is being
fabricated by means of false publicity.

> *Leonid Brezhnev, March 1977*

The idea of a sun millions of miles in diameter and
91 000 000 miles away is silly. The sun is only 32
miles across and not more than 2000 miles from
earth. It stands to reason it must be so. God made
the sun to light the earth, and therefore must have
placed it close to the task it was designed to do.
What would you think about a man who built a
house in Zion and put a lamp to light it in
Kenosha, Wisconsin?

> *Wilbur Glenn Voliva, overseer of the*
> *Christian Apostolic Church in Zion,*
> *Illinois*

I'd think he was as loony as you, bud.

I want to see peace, prosperity and happiness in my country, and I think the way we are going about it is the best way.

> *Joe Cahill, leader of the Provisional IRA*
> *on his campaign of bombings and murder,*
> *October 1971*

Mount Pelée is no more to be feared than Vesuvius in Naples.

> *Professor reassuring locals in Les Colonies,*
> *Martinique. More than 30 000 died in the*
> *1902 Mount Pelée disaster.*

It is not difficult for any cool-headed person with political understanding to see that if Hungary had not requested the assistance of Soviet troops, and if they had not assisted, Hungary today could only become a fascist hell, an imperialist outpost for overthrowing various other East European people's democracies and engineering a new world war.

> People's Daily, *Peking, on the Soviet*
> *invasion of Hungary, 1956*

Martial law might be lifted tomorrow.

> *Jerzy Ozdowski, Polish vice-premier,*
> *January 1982*

Or the next day, or the day after that, or . . . .

Lech Walesa is under 24-hour police guard for his own protection.

> *Polish government statement, June 1983*

General Hudson Austin has been taken to the helicopter carrier *Guam* for his personal protection.

> *Larry Speakes, White House Press Officer,*
> *on the capture of the man who led the*
> *Grenada coup, October 1983*

It's as safe as walking down the *Unter den Linden* in Berlin.

> *Rudolph Sauter, chief engineer on the doomed airship* Hindenburg*'s last voyage*

The real friends like the socialist countries, including the great and brotherly Soviet Union, have . . . in every circumstance, never hesitated to extend internationalist co-operation to us.

> *Barbrak Karmal of Afghanistan*

Like I said, we call them tanks.

All the plans of the community of socialist states are plans of peace and construction.

> *Yuri Andropov*

Allegations about so-called North Vietnamese forces in South Vietnam have been completely rejected.

> *Le Duc Tho, Paris, 1973*

We are only offering moral support.

> *Col. Gaddafi after his troops invaded northern Chad, 1983*

She is someone who is very intelligent and dignified. She is a very nice person.

> *Sarah Pakenham, daughter of Lord Longford, on Moors murderess Myra Hindley*

A kindly, gentle man.

> *Gertie Gitana, music hall star, on Dr Crippen*

The battle for Beirut has given us great self-confidence because it proved that Israel is weaker than we think and can be defeated militarily.

> *Yasser Arafat, January 1983*

One thing is certain, the evacuation from Beirut was not a military victory for the Israelis. As a military exercise, the Israelis suffered a humiliating defeat.

PLO London newsletter, September 1982

It's incredible how concerned you westerners are about war criminals.

Khieu Samphan, Khmer Rouge leader, asked why his men had killed four million

Apart from what is happening to me now, life is on the credit side.

Klaus Barbie, 'Butcher of Lyons', after his arrest, February 1983

But let's end on a lighter note. The astrology column of the *Surrey Comet* soared ahead in the untruth stakes with this starry-skied entry:

PISCES
Someone has gone to an awful lot of trouble to put you on the spot! Some very neat footwork on your part could well bounce it back from whence it came! Lucky birthday, February 30.

And if you'll believe that, you'll believe anything!

27
MORE U-TURNS

'Leaving was the best thing that happened to me,' said Noele Gordon in 1982. 'I woke up one morning and suddenly there was no more *Crossroads*. I felt absolutely thrilled. I was free.'

Within six months, she was saying something rather different. 'I was upset and angry. Of course I was depressed. There were days when I did not want to get out of bed in the morning.'

So, she changed her mind. It has been known to happen:

> I don't do bed scenes. I always believed what people wanted was romance, not just sex. That is what I put into *Rocky*. I would not have any nudity or grunting on a bed. I was asked to get into bed with a girl in *Farewell My Lovely* and I insisted on wearing a pair of shorts.
>
> *Sylvester Stallone, April 1977*

Unfortunately then someone turned up an old video called *Party at Kitty and Stud's* in which Mr Stallone was seen quite definitely in the buff. Said our hero:

> They wanted to know if I'd take my clothes off. Why not? I said I take them off free at home. I didn't think the movie would ever be released.
>
> *Sylvester Stallone, June 1977*

Another to U-turn was Nicki Lauda, who in October 1979 said:

> I've had enough of driving around in circles.

. . . only to return to racing.
But haven't you heard it all before?

> Segregation today – segregation tomorrow – segregation forever.
>
> *George Wallace, 1962*

I don't want segregation to come back.
> *George Wallace, 1982*

Politicians are the same the world over.

> By the end of next year, we shall be on our way to
> that so-called economic miracle we need.
>> *Denis Healey, ministerial broadcast on the*
>> *budget, April 1976*

> If we can keep our heads – and our nerve – the
> long-awaited economic miracle is in our grasp.
>> *Denis Healey, July 1976*

> No government can produce an economic miracle.
>> *Denis Healey, December 1976*

Oh dear, Denis.

> I do not think the banks had any alternative but to
> throw good money after bad in the Argentine, since
> it is probable their government would otherwise
> default on its debts.
>> *Letter to constituent, December 1982*

> Mrs Thatcher has lent the military dictatorship in
> Buenos Aires millions of pounds to buy weapons,
> including weapons made in Britain, to kill British
> servicemen. This is an act of stupefying hypocrisy.
>> *Election speech, 1 June 1983*

Hypocrisy?

> In a Reagan administration every effort will be
> made to establish and begin to implement economic
> policy early – within the first 90 days – and then
> stick to the essentials of that policy.
>> *Republican policy platform, 1980*

> We are conducting a fight within the Labour Party.
> It's not a centre party we're talking about. As long

as the two major parties do represent broad
coalitions there will be a small Liberal centre party
but no split in the Labour or Conservative parties.

> *Dr David Owen, September 1980*

I thought he was the best man for the job four
years ago. I think he's the best man for the job
today. And I'm not going to change my mind
tomorrow.

> *Richard Nixon on Spiro Agnew,*
> *Republican nomination acceptance speech,*
> *August 1972*

It actually took about a fortnight. What a difference a few
days makes.

We could end up getting married again. We
probably have the most perfect relationship in the
world.

> *Anne Turkel on Richard Harris, November*
> *1982*

He proposed; she accepted. And a few days later . . .

I am very much in love. He is going to be my next
husband.

But wait a minute – this isn't Richard Harris. It's bodybuilder
Hans Buhringer.

I don't ever expect to see her again.

> *Richard Harris on Anne Turkel, December*
> *1982*

The crossword puzzle threatens Western civilisation.
If it became widespread, it would make devastating
inroads on the working hours of every rank of
society.

> The Times, *1925*

So they made *The Times* crossword a national institution.

> I think Britain's best interests are best served by
> being in the European Community.
>
> *Roy Hattersley, July 1982*

So in 1983 he campaigned 'loyally' to pull Britain out of the
Common Market.

> I will not serve in a Labour Cabinet committed to
> unilateral disarmament or quitting NATO.
>
> *Roy Hattersley, May 1981*

So in 1983 he campaigned 'loyally' for unilateral disarmament
and the expulsion of NATO bases from Britain.

> The only real answer to the nuclear threat is multi-
> lateral disarmament and not unilateral gestures. It
> would be crazy to throw away our Polaris
> deterrent.
>
> *Denis Healey, 1981*

So in 1983 he campaigned for unilateral disarmament and the
scrapping of Polaris.

It's the same the world over – the wheels of international
politics just keep U-turning.

> At present we are trying to work out a more
> amicable relationship in government. Whatever
> breaches exist at the moment are bound to go.
>
> *Robert Mugabe on Joshua Nkomo, 1980*

> The only way to deal effectively with a snake is to
> strike and cut off its head.
>
> *Robert Mugabe on Joshua Nkomo, 1982*

It's all a struggle for power.

> Whether you believe it or not, I have anything but
> a desire to be this country's head of government.
>
> *Franz-Josef Strauss*

That's why he stood in the 1980 German election for
Chancellor.

Seven years is too long.

> *Valéry Giscard d'Estaing, on his way to*
> *the French presidency, 1974*

That's why he went on and asked for another seven. (Though the voters remembered his earlier words. They booted him out.)

As a President, Ford was pretty much of a nothing.

> *Justin Dart, interview with* Los Angeles
> Times, *February 1982*

Dear Mr President: Our country suffered greatly when we lost your leadership – witness interest rates, inflation, foreign affairs and national defense. For this very stupid reference I am sincerely embarrassed, and to be honest I am just sick about it.

> *Justin Dart, letter to Gerald Ford the very*
> *next day*

Though when it comes to the about-face, there is no doubt British is best.

The rule of law should be upheld by all political parties. They should neither advise others to break the law, nor encourage others to do so even when they strongly disagree with the legislation put forward by the Government of the day.

> *James Callaghan, 1972*

If the law is a bad law there is always the contingent right to take action that you would not otherwise take.

> *James Callaghan, 1982*

When calm returns to the industrial scene, this week's agreement between the Government and the TUC will prove to be a major turning point, which will provide the basis for a great Labour victory at the general election.

> *Joel Barnett, Chief Secretary to the*
> *Treasury, February 1979*

> To my mind, the only give and take in the social
> contract was that the Government gave, and the
> unions took.
>
> *Joel Barnett, February 1982*

But it was an American who best captured the loop-the-loop spirit of politics in one memorable quote. Daniel Moynihan resigned in 1975 as chief US delegate to the United Nations, strongly denying rumours he was going to run for the Senate:

> I would consider it dishonourable to leave this post
> and run for office and I hope that it would be
> understood that if I do, the people, the voters to
> whom I would present myself in such circumstances,
> would consider me as having said in advance that I
> am a man of no personal honour to have done so.

Needless to say, he ran. And it sums up what we have come to expect from our politicians – he won, too.

28
MORE EXCUSES

'Lying,' wrote Samuel Butler, 'has a kind of respect and reverence with it. We pay the person a compliment of acknowledging his superiority whenever we lie to him.' Said H.L. Mencken: 'It is hard to believe that a man is telling the truth when you know that you would lie if you were in his place.' Or, as Adlai Stevenson put it: 'A lie is an abomination to the Lord. And a very present help in trouble.'

Some more weasel words . . . .

> I never thought of myself as a wicked brothel-keeper – I thought of myself as a welfare worker.
>
> *Mrs Cynthia Payne*

My brothers have been represented as mindless thugs with a propensity for violence and little else. It is a completely false picture. They lacked higher education, true, but more than made up for that in personality . . . and wit. They met with the famous and the notorious and were able to hold their own in any company. They dealt with their problems decisively and effectively, a phrase which may serve as a fitting epitaph some time in the distant future.

> *Charles Kray, brother of the notorious*
> *London gangster-killers*

We might have lost the game, but we won in the bath.

> *Rugger saying*

My tactics were right, I wouldn't change them. The trouble was the players didn't play after the first 15 minutes or so.

> *Scots soccer manager Ally McLeod, after*
> *shock World Cup defeat by Peru*

Exactly what I wanted.

> *Sergei Diaghilev, after rioting at first*
> *performance of Stravinsky's* Rite of Spring

While I may have been guilty of errors in judgment, while I may have crossed over the line which divides appropriate service to constituents from excessive boasting and posturing, I have never engaged in any illegal conduct; I never corrupted my office.

> *Sen. Harrison 'Pete' Williams, convicted in*
> *the Abscam case of bribery and*
> *conspiracy, to Senate ethics committee*

Oh no?

Some have been nauseated by the words, many others have criticised them as not being in good taste, particularly because in one line I say 'God bless Martin Bormann'. But my objective was to show that if we are going to live in and make a better Christian society, then we must start with some basic tenets, and the most fundamental of these is forgiveness for everyone. We cannot discriminate between Martin Bormann and the

Good Samaritan if we are to live our lives in a Christian world.

Ronald Biggs, on making a record with the punk group, the Sex Pistols

Excuses are, of course, the constant resort of traders, and officials anxious to 'fob off' the public.

Two weeks after J.C. Francis of Otley moved into his new home, the bathroom sink cracked. An official told him:

You've been running hot water in it, haven't you!

While Mrs Winifred Etteridge, of Croydon, found that the ribs on her new umbrella had gone rusty and stained the fabric. Taking it back to the shop she was told sternly:

This article must have been out in the wet.

After one family moved into a council house at St Albans, Herts, a black mould appeared on the ceiling. A council official told them:

You know, you shouldn't cook in the kitchen.

Why do people do it?

> I didn't kill for a year. Mental anguish.
> > *Peter Sutcliffe, the Yorkshire Ripper*

> I felt within myself a need to be perfect.
> > *Janet Cooke, who faked a* Washington
> > Post *story and won a Pulitzer prize*

Ah, perfection.

> Do I live the life of a good socialist . . . the
> champagne socialist question. I'd ask myself: is that
> very inconsistent with one's beliefs? I don't know. I
> sent my daughter to private school, for instance.
> What would I say? Well, we live in a rat race: what
> alternatives have you got?
> > *John Mortimer QC*

> I promised I'd take Rotherham out of the Second
> Division. I did . . . into the Third Division.
> > *Tommy Docherty*

After a 14-year-old girl and her 15-year-old boyfriend shot
dead the girl's mother, 41-year-old Mrs Anna Rivera, so they
could get married, a New York detective spokesman said:

> It's a modern-day love story. It's a Romeo and
> Juliet type of thing.

But the police are funny about such things. A 19-year-old
housewife from Memphis told a grand jury she had had sex
with 5000 policemen in three years. Her excuse:

> After an hour and a half trapped in a sauna bath I
> changed from a devout Catholic housewife into a
> nymphomaniac.

Mind you, it must be awful to be incarcerated.

After he was caught 'on the run' from Borstal, Arthur
Brazier, 18, told Wolverhampton magistrates:

Life was too easy there. There's no discipline at all
and I started getting relaxed and idle. That's the
reason I ran away.

He added:

The taxpayer ought to find out about this.

There are lapses on the other side of the law, sure enough.
Members of a jury at Canterbury Crown Court in September
1982 were told they would not be able to see the exhibits in an
armed robbery case. Said Mr Andrew Goymer, prosecuting:

Unfortunately they have all been eaten by the police
dog.

Though undoubtedly the most pertinent – and
honest – excuse ever was that once given by Governor Earl
Long of Louisiana.
Immediately after being elected on a pledge to cut taxes, the
larger-than-life Governor sent the State legislature a bill
calling for a tax hike.
When an aide protested that what he was doing was
outrageous, he had just been elected on a promise to do
exactly the opposite, Governor Long shrugged his shoulders
and said:

I lied.

29
TWENTY-FOUR EXPLANATIONS NEVER TO GIVE TO THE POLICE

It's the time, sooner or later, we all need a handy lie. But remember there are good lies and bad lies. If stopped by the police, whatever you do, DON'T say:

1 I collect wheel clamps – you should see how many I've got at home.
2 I needed the clamp to keep the mother-in-law out of the way for the weekend.
3 I'm a hit man for the Libyan People's Bureau, and I claim dyslexic immunity.
4 I'm on my way to play strip poker with the Chief Constable.
5 I'm on my way to a gangland execution.
6 Insurance? What insurance?
7 I don't need a driver's licence. I never took my test.
8 It's only the third police car I've hit this week.
9 Of course I know it's a one way street. Every other fool was driving the wrong way.
10 I was confused by all those blue flashing lights behind me, so I drove faster to get out of their way.
11 You see, I travel in ladies' undergarments and it can be very uncomfortable driving in hot weather.
12 I can only think I must have stood in some superglue and my foot stuck to the accelerator.
13 I was just testing what your old jalopy would do.
14 I always top the ton in bandit country.
15 We've got to get the world land speed record back one day.
16 Every time I see a road sign to Nottingham, I think I'm Steve McQueen.
17 I thought red lights meant naughty women ahead, so I put my foot down and drove straight through.
18 I was rushing to the police station to report a maniac driver.

19   I was rushing home to try and catch *Police Five* on TV.

20   I've got a helmet like yours at home, my brother brought it back from a football match.

21   I could have done 120, but I'm a bit wary at the moment because the tyres are all bald.

22   I didn't know I was speeding. I was fast asleep at the wheel.

23   I couldn't read the speedometer anyhow – I've had far too much to drink.

24   It's OK, it's not even my car. I just saw it outside the pub with the keys in. I hope the owner won't get into trouble.

30
DOUBLE STANDARDS, DOUBLETHINK

'The theft of books from public libraries has become alarmingly frequent,' wrote master traitor Anthony Blunt. 'I won't ride horses. I think they are dangerous,' said superstar bike crash victim Barry Sheene.

Barry Goldwater was another. 'I think brinkmanship is a pretty good word,' he said, telling how he wanted to 'let Castro have it' and drop an atom bomb on the Chinese supply lines to Vietnam. Then, in much the same breath, he added: 'I have never considered myself an extremist.'

In *1984* George Orwell called it doublethink – the capacity to hold two completely contradictory views, and to believe simultaneously in both of them.

> Every government, every country, has the right to exercise force where necessary. For instance, in the name of unity.
>
> *Zulfikar Ali Bhutto, President of Pakistan, 1972*

His successors took him at his word. They hanged him.

> We are prepared to fight for peace.
>
> *Margaret Thatcher, TV press conference with Chancellor Kohl of West Germany, February 1983*

> Sure pro-football is violent. That's one of the nicest things about it.
>
> *George Blanda, pro-football star*

> Just stay single for a while.
>
> *Prince Charles to Linda McLean, 21, and Amanda McShannon, 17, while touring a Scottish canning factory, 1982*

> I'm very fond of my pigs. But I don't find it difficult to eat them.
>
> *Robert Runcie, Archbishop of Canterbury*

I wasn't happy when the umpire told the spectators to be quiet. It only encourages them to make more noise.

John McEnroe, Wimbledon 1982

Perhaps the greatest exponent of the art in recent years has been Willie (now Lord) Whitelaw, with his famous 'Willyisms'.

They are going round the country stirring up complacency.

On Labour ministers, 1974

When offered a drink by a local party worker Mr Whitelaw nodded:

I will have a little whisky.

He then became rather tetchy. His host didn't understand why. Finally he explained:

When I say I would like a little whisky, I mean I would like a large one, thank you very much.

Though the most famous 'Willyism' came when Mr Whitelaw was Secretary for Ulster, and he pronounced on IRA parades:

I have always thought it a great mistake ever to prejudge the past.

Doublethink has been a fairly common phenomenon in the run up to 1984.

Germany is not only an island of peace – she is an armed island of peace.

Dr Joseph Goebbels, 1936

Peace for the people of Vietnam is the purpose for our presence in Vietnam.

Lyndon B. Johnson

LABOUR ISN'T WORKING.

> *Conservative election poster by Saatchi and*
> *Saatchi, 1979*

Mr Mackenzie never talks to the press.

> *Spokesman for* Sun *editor Kelvin*
> *Mackenzie after another Press Council*
> *complaint*

He declared himself always available – then there was a sign on his door saying 'No Admittance'.

> *Sue Tanswell, secretary at NUM*
> *headquarters, on Arthur Scargill*

I'm no playboy. What is a playboy anyway?

> *Prince Andrew*

I can't answer any more questions. I still remain under the Official Secrets Act.

> *Anthony Blunt press conference,*
> *November 1979*

It never seemed to bother you before.

The suspects were found in a car on spare land in Bradford with a dagger on the seat, two more in a holdall and a machete in a suitcase. Wilkins told police officers: 'We are going to London on a Ban the Bomb march.'

> *Court report in the* Daily Telegraph

DAVID DIMBLEBY: Are you satisfied with the methods SAVAK use to get confessions?
SHAH OF IRAN: They are improving every day.

> Panorama, *BBC-TV*

Turn the screw until it bleeds, then turn it again . . . . We want you for ever, please don't go away.

> *Sir Freddie Laker to Margaret Thatcher,*
> *June 1980*

It's all yours, you can have it! Your wonderful
democracy! You'll see in a few years, where your
wonderful democracy leads!

Shah of Iran, 1973

This country is in a terrible state and it is only the
people that can put it right by hard work and
dedication. We have to put in a lot more hours and
a lot more effort.

Don Revie, England soccer manager, 1975

So he left for a job in the United Arab Emirates.
   Mind you, Tommy Docherty did say:

Any soccer manager who says he has not cheated or
lied is not being honest.

The moderate members of our party must stand up
and be counted.

Reg Prentice, Labour MP

So he left to join the Tories.

I personally am shocked that Michael Foot has not
continued the fight he himself started.

Robert Mellish on Foot and Tatchell

But he'd already left the Labour Party.

Everyone in the Liberal Party is in favour of the
Alliance. It's just that we don't like the SDP.

*David Blunt, Liberal candidate for South-
East Cornwall*

I favour capital punishment. It saves lives.

Nancy Reagan

Of course we are not patronising women. We are
just going to explain to them in words of one
syllable what it is all about.

*Lady Olga Maitland, founder of 'Women
for Peace'*

Finally to Republican Congressman Richard Kelly, of Florida. After admitting accepting 25 000 dollars from FBI agents posing as Arab sheiks in what came to be known as the 'Abscam' case, Mr Kelly (who was later convicted of fraud and resigned) claimed:

> I was conducting my own investigation of shady characters.

Yet he had not told any law agency, had used the money as petty cash, and had returned the balance to the FBI only when he'd been named in the case. Not surprisingly, he was asked to take a lie detector test.

Said Mr Kelly:

> Absolutely not. I don't trust them.

31
ALL'S UNTRUE THAT ENDS UNTRUE

'A more humble, unassuming little man I have never met,' said Dr Gilbert W. Rylance, partner in a dental practice with Dr Hawley Harvey Crippen. 'The young man was what might mercifully be described as inadequate,' wrote critic Alexander Woollcott, after witnessing the first stage performance of one Humphrey Bogart. 'I think I'll last longer than anyone else who's governed Pakistan,' said Zulfikar Ali Bhutto in 1972.

Truth will, most definitely, out.

Beware the lie that stands revealed in the fullness of time.

> I was subjected to the close, critical reporting that is a tradition in American politics . . . yet Mr Nixon escaped similar scrutiny.
>
> *George McGovern, 1972*

But not for long.

> I was not built for standby equipment, and under no circumstances will I be a candidate for the Vice-Presidency.
>
> *Nelson Rockefeller, later V-P under Ford*

> Whatever excuses the Prime Minister may give, he cannot run away from the fact that our policies did not produce unemployment as his have. He will go down in history as the Prime Minister for Unemployment.
>
> *Margaret Thatcher to James Callaghan, 1978, when unemployment was 1.5 million. Her Government doubled it.*

> Knowing full well the responsibilities that devolve on a Prime Minister, and how difficult it is to cater to all requirements of a nation and satisfy them, I will not accept the post of Premier even if it is offered me.
>
> *Mrs Sirimavo Bandaranaike of Ceylon, 1958*

179

It was offered, she accepted, and became the world's first woman Prime Minister.

> It isn't a book I would gamble on for a big sale. But I'm sure one can be sure of 10 000 anyway.
>
> *George Orwell on* 1984

> The people are as quiet and submissive to government as any people under the sun; and as little inclined to tumults, riots, seditions, as they were ever known to be since the first foundations of Government. The repeal of the Stamp Act has composed every wave of popular disorder into a smooth and peaceful calm.
>
> *John Adams, 1766, on why there wouldn't be an American revolution*

> Let us throw hypocrisy to the winds. In Andrew Boyle's *Climate of Treason*, which describes but does not name two senior 'moles', the real position is as follows. 'Maurice' is Sir Anthony Blunt, formerly keeper of the Queen's pictures and a distinguished historian in his own right . . . . Both men, as far as anybody can tell, are wholly innocent.
>
> *Christopher Hitchens, New Statesman, November 1979*

> You can mark down 25 June 1978 as the day Scottish football conquers the world. For that Sunday, I am convinced, the finest team that Scotland has produced can play in the World Cup Final in Buenos Aires . . . and WIN. I'm so sure we can do it that I give my permission here and now for the big celebration on June 25 to be made an annual festival – a national Ally-day.
>
> *Ally McLeod, Scottish soccer boss. Scotland were knocked out in the opening round of the World Cup Finals in Argentina*

I am 1000 per cent for Tom Eagleton and I have no intention of dropping him from the ticket.
> *George McGovern, July 1972*

George, before you change your mind, I accept.
> *Tom Eagleton, July 1972*

Within hours, he was dropped from the ticket.

The President has no intention of resigning. He has every intention of fulfilling the vitally important objectives he has set for the nation and for himself.
> *Gerald Warren, spokesman for Richard Nixon, November 1973*

The economic crisis, with the unpopular measures it has demanded, is now virtually over. The future is bright with promise.
> *Harold Wilson, February 1965*

We're on the eve of destruction.
> *Barry McGuire, song title, 1963*

Artillery only seems effective against raw troops. Cavalry will have a larger sphere of action in future wars.
> *Earl Haig, 1914*

SOPHIE TIPPED TO OUST KOO
Ex-deb Sophie Birdwood is being tipped as the new girl in Prince Andrew's life after spending the weekend at Balmoral.
> Daily Mirror, *August 1983*

KOO! ANDREW'S GOT A NEW GIRL
Prince Andrew has a new girlfriend leaving soft porn actress Koo Stark out in the cold. The girl in his life now is former Deb of the Year the Honourable Sophie Birdwood, who looks remarkably like Princess Diana.
> Daily Express, *August 1983*

ANDY'S GIRL
This is the girl who spent the weekend with Prince
Andrew at Balmoral. She is blonde society beauty
the Hon. Sophie Birdwood, 19.

> Daily Star, *August 1983*

It wasn't her. Poor Sophie was on her way back from holiday
in the Bahamas. She said, 'I don't find it very funny. I don't
know Prince Andrew or Koo Stark and I don't know who this
girl is they say is me.' In fact it was Lady Carolyn Herbert,
daughter of the Queen's racing manager, Lord Porchester,
and a long time friend of the Royal Family.

> The Communists turn their attention chiefly to
> Germany because that country is on the eve of a
> bourgeois revolution that will be the prelude to an
> immediately following proletarian revolution.
>
> *Karl Marx,* The Communist Manifesto

> I do wish it might be possible to get at any rate *The
> Times*, Camrose, Beaverbrook Press etc to write up
> Hitler as the apostle of peace. It will be terribly
> short-sighted if this is not done.
>
> *Sir Neville Henderson, British Ambassador
> to Berlin, 1938*

> What we have done hasn't been a sellout. It has
> been to give South Vietnam an opportunity to
> survive in conditions that, today, are more political
> than military.
>
> *Henry Kissinger, 1972*

And more temporary than permanent.

> The army will remain only 25 miles inside Lebanon
> purely as an international arrangement to prevent
> terrorists from establishing artillery positions within
> range of the border.
>
> *Shimon Peres, Israeli Opposition leader,
> June 1982*

I have no desire to get back into politics if I lose this time.

Barry Goldwater, May 1964

Though he just might go back to the Senate.

'Steady Ed' Muskie . . . eschews flamboyancy, but has a fine, granite-like persona.

The Times, *January 1972*

Except when he's crying.

It was a victory for a mild, popular, highly-cultured man . . . the man who for decades had been portrayed by the press as a wild, long-haired, Marxist extremist, and who had now, suddenly and unexpectedly, emerged as the possible next Prime Minister.

*Simon Hoggart and David Leigh on
Michael Foot's election as Labour leader*

We are the heart of the party. We are what the Labour movement is all about. We are going to win and we are going to keep it that way.

*William Rodgers MP, on being a Labour
moderate, 1977*

If I got fed up with the Labour Party, I should leave politics altogether.

Shirley Williams, 1979

Japan is not capable of war on a great scale. Japan represents a reservoir of a great revolutionary explosion.

Leon Trotsky, 1939

The Tories are roaring ahead, Labour are floundering badly.

Daily Express, *February 1974*

The NUM will certainly win this one.

> *Arthur Scargill, before humiliating vote*
> *against him by his members, October 1982*

We'll win.

> *Sir Alec Douglas-Home, October 1964*

As I have kept saying, Labour will certainly win.

> *Robert Carvel,* Evening Standard, *June*
> *1970*

We're definitely going to win. No doubt about it.

> *Rosalynn Carter, October 1980*

The tougher it gets, the more determined he
becomes to get the truth out and to weather this
thing.

> *Alexander Haig on Nixon, November 1973*

I fully expect to resume my duties.

> *Richard Allen, November 1981; five weeks*
> *later, Allen, President Reagan's National*
> *Security Advisor, resigned over a $1000*
> *gift from Japanese journalists who*
> *interviewed Nancy Reagan*

Thank you, doctors, thank you, nurses, I'll be all
right in a few days.

> *Alfred I. Du Pont, dying words*

I don't mind what anyone calls me. There is a
budget to be balanced now, and that's what I'm
going to do, no matter what.

> *David Stockman, US Budget Director, July*
> *1981*

I will continue – I intend to continue in office.

> *Cecil Parkinson, MP, after revealing that*
> *his secretary, Sarah Keays, was expecting*
> *his child, October 1983*

32
I NEVER THOUGHT IT WOULD END LIKE THIS

'Momma still thinks I'm the smartest of her boys,' mused Billy Carter when Jimmy went to the White House. 'I'm basically a home body at heart,' said Margaret Trudeau.

And famous English composer Sir William Walton confided: 'You know, sometimes I don't even like music.'

They can't have said it. Or can they?

And yes, they did say:

> She's just like the lady next door.
>
> *Easterhouse, Glasgow, housewife on*
> *Princess Diana*

> If I had my life to live over again, I'd be a plumber.
>
> *Albert Einstein*

> Me, I just act natural.
>
> *Jimmy Connors*

> I am a realist.
>
> *Pulp Western king J.T. Edson*

> Every night when I go to bed I ask myself: 'What did I do today that we can point to for the future generations to come to say that we laid the foundation for a more peaceful and prosperous world?'
>
> *Lyndon B. Johnson*

> We've got to look over our institutions and return them to the old values.
>
> *Richard Nixon, 1972*

> Art? Art? All the art in the world isn't worth a good meat and potato pie.
>
> *L.S. Lowry*

The Labour Party should not be afraid of revisionism and being told our socialism has ceased to become full-blooded.

> *William Rodgers MP*

I saw the match on TV, but I must confess I didn't recognise her.

> *Frank Westwood, employer of Twickenham streaker Erika Roe*

I never thought it would end like this.

> *Robert Chatwin, who disappeared to Spain at the same time as £3 million in gems, when arrested by police*

I was a near hopeless haemophiliac Liberal. I bled for causes. I had voted Democratic in every election . . . I was blindly and busily joining every organisation I could find that would guarantee to save the world.

> *Ronald Reagan – yes, Ronald Reagan – in* Where's the Rest of Me?

Overexposing Ronald Reagan as President is like overexposing Bo Derek.

> *Sen. Paul Laxalt*

Yes, I am rather prudish.

> *Mandy Rice-Davies*

And I'm Adolf Hitler.

Kissing Marilyn Monroe was like kissing Adolf Hitler.

> *Tony Curtis*

One question: how on earth does he know?

I have offered my hand to Britain again and again. It was the very essence of my programme to come to terms. We have never demanded anything from them. I have repeatedly offered them my hand, but always in vain.

Adolf Hitler

The Soviet army is a special kind of army, a school that fosters feelings of brotherhood, solidarity and mutual respect among all Soviet nations and nationalities. Our armed forces are one friendly family.

Leonid Brezhnev

By 1984, a newspaper delivered by van or pushed through the letter box will have become a preposterous anachronism.

Sir Gerald Barry, Granada TV boss, 1964

I am at the height of my career. I am in my political prime.

Norman St John-Stevas, one time Cabinet minister, now back-bencher, 1983

South Africa has always been a place where we have proper and clean administration.

P.W. Botha

We now have a Rhodesian constitution, and if anybody knows where it can be improved, I would like to know.

Ian Smith

There were one or two helpful suggestions.

We needn't worry now about the possibility of going into Europe.

Harold Wilson, 1966

I don't want the part for money, marbles, or chalk.
Clark Gable, turning down Rhett Butler in
Gone With The Wind

By-election ever-present Bill Boakes said when losing yet another deposit in the February 1974 contest:

> If I had been elected, I think I would have been the next Prime Minister.

> The fact is we have got Stalingrad.
> *Adolf Hitler, 1942*

> Nobody ever tells the truth about me.
> *John McEnroe*

> I'm incapable of telling a joke.
> *Eric Morecambe*

> These are lies, and just because a lie is repeated many times it is nonetheless still a lie.
> *Victor Issraelyan, Soviet arms negotiator at Geneva, February 1983*

Well, your lot should certainly know about that.

> All I know is that I'm not a Marxist.
> *Karl Marx*

> Iran is an island of stability in one of the most volatile parts of the world.
> *Jimmy Carter*

> This was just an ordinary flight, except that it was longer.
> *Amy Johnson on flying solo to Australia*

> It is a perfectly ordinary little case of a man charged with indecency with four or five guardsmen.
> *Mervyn Griffiths-Jones, London prosecuting counsel*

> I think that being an Old Etonian can be an embarrassment, a cross a boy has to bear probably all his life.
> *Anthony Chenevix-Trench, Headmaster of Eton, 1964*

It taught me such a lot, being at Harrow. You meet such a cross-section of society there.

Andrew Nelson, MP

I am an ordinary kind of chap.

Patrick Moore

I have no ego, none at all. Getting rid of your ego is critical to a man's development.

Malcolm Allison

People have the wrong impression. He really is a very kind man.

'Major' Bob Astles on Idi Amin

New Zealand is the birthplace of the twentieth century.

Prof. Frank Parsons

If I were a teenager today, I'd probably be a pink-haired punk.

Mrs Mary Whitehouse

I think I'm a very sensitive flower really.

Denis Healey

My burning desire is to be a monk.

Richard Harris

As a manager I've got a habit of saying the right things.

Ally McLeod

I didn't actually realise before that babies were born without a soundproof wing and a nanny. It didn't occur to me there was any other way.

Roddy Llewelyn

Peace has broken out in the Labour Party.

David Basnett, Bishop's Stortford, January 1982

The world is much more primitive that it was fifty years ago. Scientific and technical progress could not survive in a strictly regimented society.

George Orwell, 1984

I'm a pretty quiet sort of a bloke really.

Jeff 'Terror' Thomson

The beautiful doesn't matter to me.

Pablo Picasso

Only a fool wants a confrontation, and only a fool wants a strike.

Arthur Scargill

The Queen's bedroom door is always guarded by a uniformed policeman.

Craig Brown and Lesley Cunliffe, The Book of Royal Lists

Except when there are intruders about.

Tennis players are very sensitive people.

John McEnroe

I want to earn an honest living.

Ronald Biggs

Let's see if I can work the magic here again.
Ally McLeod on joining Motherwell (he didn't)

Finally, I think the Shah of Iran spoke for everyone in the world of forked tongues when he said, in a classic quote:

I really have everything. My life goes forward like a beautiful dream.

THE COMPULSIVE LIARS'
INTERNATIONAL BROTHERHOOD

The International Brotherhood of Compulsive Liars exists on nine continents for the furtherance of lying, cheating, and rank deception.

Hon. President: Idi Amin Dada, V.C., M.C., D.D., Defender of the Faith, Conqueror of the British Empire, Emeritus Professor of English at the University of Oxford, over 1000 appearances on radio and TV inc. David Frost show, Punchlines, Crossroads, Game for a Laugh
Hon. Vice-Presidents: Col. Muammar Gaddafi, Ayatollah Khomeini, J.R. Ewing
Hon. Secretary: G. Jones

The Brotherhood is pleased to announce that the membership register is now open for a limited period.

Members of these professions qualify for IMMEDIATE FREE MEMBERSHIP:

> Members of Parliament
> US Congressmen
> Master spies
> PR executives
> International hit-men
> Advertising executives
> Journalists
> Used car salesmen
> Presidents and ex-Presidents of the USA

Other applicants must offer evidence of successful deception in one of the following areas:

> Cheating in school examinations
> Acquittal in court of law after totally perjured evidence
> Cheating spouse or income tax authorities over a
>   minimum five year period
> Accepting bribes then successfully denying it

Voting for one candidate after accepting lift in rival
    candidate's car
Showing enthusiasm for Ronald Reagan TV broadcast
   or Eurovision Song Contest

I am a liar because . . . .

You must in addition supply three totally bogus references:

And a completely invented name and address:

    False name _____

    False address _____

    _____

    _____ False postcode _____

Enclose a forged cheque or counterfeit cash for £5.50 or
equivalent and send to: International Brotherhood of
Compulsive Liars, c/o Graham Jones, Kingsmead, Barnet,
Hertfordshire EN5 5AY.

You will receive, by return, a copy of the Brotherhood's rules and regulations; a phoney Order of Lenin medal and Yale University graduation certificate; the current issue of our monthly magazine 'The Plain Untruth', and a framed, life-sized portrait of Tommy Docherty. There is 150% off basic subscriptions for employees of the CIA, the home civil service, and previous members of Argentine juntas.